Pastor Conlon is my pastor. When I first heard about him, he pastored a small church up in Canada. He had been a former police officer, and the Lord got ahold of his life. Leonard Ravenhill had said, "You need to hear this young man." I heard one tape, and then I put on the other. Halfway through the Lord said, "Call him." I pulled the car off the road...and I called. When he got up to preach, I said, "That's a God-touched man. That's a man of God." And our hearts were one.

—DAVID WILKERSON
FOUNDING PASTOR, TIMES SQUARE CHURCH
BEST-SELLING AUTHOR, *THE CROSS AND THE SWITCHBLADE*

Carter has taught us much, but most of all he has taught us to pray. I've been challenged and blessed by his teaching and example. You will be as well.

—MAX LUCADO
PASTOR; BEST-SELLING AUTHOR

Over the decades, I've spoken in many hundreds of churches, but none quite like Times Square Church. At 6:00 a.m. scores of believers gathered to begin praying for the Sunday service, long before I was scheduled to speak. As I wheeled to the platform, never had I felt so enveloped, so supported by such dynamic prayer! It's obvious that Pastor Conlon's life is woven in and out with praise and intercession—and in his new book, *It's Time to Pray*, he imparts to the reader the same passion and enthusiasm for prayer that he does to every member of his church. In short, prayer changes everything, and if you wish to know a greater intimacy with Christ, as well as a deeper experience of His power, this is the book for you. I highly recommend it!

—JONI EARECKSON TADA
FOUNDER, JONI AND FRIENDS INTERNATIONAL
DISABILITY CENTER

Pastor Conlon knows the power of prayer firsthand. His own

life is Exhibit A. In *It's Time to Pray* he weaves together his testimony with biblical examples and dynamic teaching to form a tapestry of truth to awaken Christ followers to the freedom of abundant life.

—ANNE GRAHAM LOTZ
FOUNDER, ANGEL MINISTRIES
BEST-SELLING AUTHOR

Carter Conlon does not call us to prayer casually. He explains in his new book, *It's Time to Pray*, how the Lord has given him visions of difficult and challenging times ahead. Pastor Carter is aware of the potential suffering he might personally suffer for proclaiming Jesus Christ as Lord. I have often stood with head bowed and hands raised at Times Square Church as Pastor Carter led his congregation in heartfelt, earnest prayers for the lost, for the heartbroken, for the sick, for a new generation of seekers, and especially for revival among the churches that must bring a saving knowledge of Jesus Christ to refugees from the difficult times and spiritual challenges that are so close at hand. I am blessed beyond measure to have a friend in Carter Conlon. I am even more blessed to have Carter Conlon as my pastor—a man of God who boldly proclaims, "It is time to pray!"

—JOHN HOOVER
NEW YORK TIMES BEST-SELLING AUTHOR

Action without prayer is like driving a car without an engine. The reality is you have no power to go anywhere! My good friend Pastor Carter Conlon helps us understand the powerful, life-changing truth that Jesus shared with His disciples in Mark 9 and how it applies to us. It's time to start your engine—pray!

—TONY PERKINS
PRESIDENT, FAMILY RESEARCH COUNCIL
PRESIDENT, COUNCIL FOR NATIONAL POLICY

IT'S TIME TO
PRAY

IT'S TIME TO
PRAY

CARTER CONLON

GPC
BOOKS
PS68:11

CHARISMA
HOUSE

Most CHARISMA HOUSE BOOK GROUP products are available at special quantity discounts for bulk purchase for sales promotions, premiums, fund-raising, and educational needs. For details, write Charisma House Book Group, 600 Rinehart Road, Lake Mary, Florida 32746, or telephone (407) 333-0600.

IT'S TIME TO PRAY by Carter Conlon
Published by GPC Books, a division of Times Square Church, in partnership with Charisma House

Charisma Media/Charisma House Book Group
600 Rinehart Road
Lake Mary, Florida 32746
www.charismahouse.com

Visit the author's website at carterconlon.com.

Library of Congress Cataloging-in-Publication Data:
An application to register this book for cataloging has been submitted to the Library of Congress.
International Standard Book Number: 978-1-62999-578-6
E-book ISBN: 978-1-62999-583-0

19 20 21 22 23 — 7 6 5 4 3
Printed in the United States of America

To Jason, Jared, and Kate, may you always be known for faith and remembered for kindness.

Much love, Dad

CONTENTS

ACKNOWLEDGMENTS

FIRST CORINTHIANS 12:14 says, "For in fact the body is not one member but many." I want to thank all of you who gave of your heart and talent to encourage the body of Christ to be renewed in prayer. To John Hoover, Melinda Ronn, Luly McCoy, Kate Hughes, Teresa Conlon, David Leonard, and Tammy Shannon, my most heartfelt thanks! Your help was invaluable. We did it in unity of heart and purpose. Psalm 133 gives the promise that where brethren dwell together in unity, God Himself commands a blessing of life. May this work spark a renewal of prayer in people's hearts, bringing the blessing of God again into our homes, our families, our towns, our communities, and our nation.

FOREWORD

IN THE SUMMER of 1988 I was born again. I lived in Darien, Connecticut, and immediately began attending an amazing church there called St. Paul's. The preaching was extraordinary, and the worship was powerful. The people who attended believed in miracles and prayed for miracles, and God often performed miracles. Many people had their lives changed there. But no sooner had I settled in than the Charismatic and brilliant pastor who had been at the center of this movement decided it was finally time to retire. I was devastated. Was it perhaps time for me to leave too? If I needed help deciding whether to stay, a woman with whom I had just broken up after a long relationship decided that she would continue attending. So perhaps it was indeed best for me to move on. But where would I go? What could compare to this spectacular place?

My friend Joey Somma had the answer to my problems. "You've got to come to Times Square Church with us!" he said. "It's like totally nuts!" (Joey actually spoke that way then.) I found it hard to believe that there was any church as wonderful as Joey maintained, but he was relentless in getting me to come. "Have you ever heard of David Wilkerson?" he asked. "He wrote *The Cross and the Switchblade*! You've got to read it!" So I quickly read *The Cross and the Switchblade* and was smitten with it—with the outrageous and true story of a young, skinny country preacher sent by God into the most dangerous parts of New York in the late 1950s with the goal of reaching the hardened gang members with the message of Jesus. It was a story of miracles upon miracles. And Joey was telling me that this same fiery country preacher had just started a church in Manhattan, thirty years later?

So one day in the spring of 1990 I drove from New Canaan, Connecticut, into Manhattan and stepped into the landmark Broadway theater that was now Times Square Church. It was magnificently ornate, with red velvet seats and gilded columns and ornate theater boxes. But the decor was nothing compared with what happened once the heavy curtain rose to the rafters and the worship began. I'd never seen anything like it. The church was filled with over fifteen hundred people of every nationality and color and background—including a liberal sprinkling of street people and former drug addicts—and everyone was singing and shouting and leaping and laughing. In other words, the joint was jumping!

And in the pulpit to preach as fiery a message as I had ever heard was none other than David Wilkerson. But the skinny country preacher from the paperback classic had been transformed into a sixty-year-old, no less wild-eyed for God than he was in the book I had just read! When it was all over and I walked out onto the streets of Manhattan, I felt palpably different about the whole city. It couldn't be the same city anymore—not after what I had experienced. If all that was going on in a theater in the middle of Times Square, New York was simply not the same and never again could be. God was in New York.

I was so moved by what I saw that evening that I soon decided to attend regularly. Two or three times a week a group of us would drive down from Connecticut. Even when I wasn't able to attend a service, I would listen to cassette tapes in my car of one of the sermons I had missed. A whole new world had been opened for me, and my faith grew and grew, like a beanstalk soaring through the clouds to touch heaven itself. Over the next years I met many new friends there. Then one weekend in 1994 I met Susanne, the woman I would marry.

That same year a new pastor arrived at Times Square Church. He was a young man from rural Canada, a former cop named Carter Conlon. David Wilkerson's younger brother Don was also a pastor at the church, and one day he asked his son Todd (now my radio announcer!) if Todd and I could take Pastor Carter's teenage sons out for a bite after the service to be hospitable. So we did. We took them right next door to Beefsteak Charlie's—today it's a McDonald's!—and had some food and talked. But what did two New Yorkers in their twenties say to teenagers from the wilds of Canada? Did you guess that we talked about hockey? We did. Little did I dream then that that brand-new pastor would grow into the extraordinary man of God that he is, genuinely humble and loving and a spiritual father to so many—that he, in fact, would become the senior pastor of the church and would be leading its flock nearly a quarter of a century later.

Two years later Susanne and I got married, and Don Wilkerson performed the service. And then life somehow took the two of us to a number of other churches. But whenever we went back to visit Times Square Church, it was precisely the same. The worship and preaching were as powerful as anything I'd ever experienced. In 2009 I went through a particularly tough patch of life—including depression—and I needed help, so I decided to go back to Times Square Church every Tuesday night. The preaching and the worship in all their fire and joy were precisely as they had been fifteen years earlier. I was astounded and deeply grateful. I found the presence of God there during those services in a way that I desperately needed, and week by week I clung to God and slowly climbed out of my deep pit.

Many times before the services I would do what many people have done for years and still do today. I would go right up to the altar—which is the theater stage—and shut my eyes and pray. If it's possible to feel an anointing—and of course it is—I always felt the anointing of God there. The prayers that have gone up to heaven from that sanctuary since it opened are beyond counting. But I also know that all those on the pastoral staff and in other parts of Times Square Church are devoted to prayer. You cannot fake that—though some have tried—and the consistency of God's presence there is a testament to that day-in-and-day-out reality.

Now, all these years later, I have been given the great honor and privilege of sometimes preaching from that blessed pulpit. And by God's grace the services and the joy and presence of God are still just the same at Times Square Church as they were the day I walked into that building nearly thirty years ago. I've been to hundreds of churches, but in all this time I simply have never experienced anything quite like Times Square Church. This is not to say that there aren't extra-ordinary churches elsewhere, but the grittiness and despair that one finds rather dramatically in evidence in New York, combined with the desperation of many of those who have attended, create an atmosphere in which one is utterly un-interested in playing church, in which prayers are earnest and powerful, and gratitude—expressed in worship—is similarly earnest and powerful. Over all these years it is still the same. At nearly every service people weep and others literally leap for joy.

If we ask what makes Times Square Church what it is, there can be only one answer—and the pastors there have been saying it since the church opened in 1987. It is prayer. That's it. You can't worship the way they do and preach the way they do and see lives changed the way they do without prayer. It's at the heart of the miraculous transformation of every life committed to following Jesus. And it is at the heart of everything else worth talking about.

So I wish everyone I know could experience what I have experienced at Times Square Church, could see that holiness and joy are two sides of the same coin, could see that worshipping God can be the most honest and beautiful and joyful thing you will ever do, could see that fervent prayer is part of the normal Christian life and that without it we are less than who God made us to be. Attending Times Square Church can be one way to see all those things. But if you can't attend there, or even visit, how wonderful it would be if the man whom God has used all these years to lead this church would write a book on the principal component behind what God is doing in that church—on prayer!

Well, by God's grace that man—whom I'm deeply privileged to call a friend—has done just that. And you are holding it in your hands. This book is the fruit of a life poured out in love for Jesus and for others. May the God who loves you and longs for your prayers use it to transform you as others have been transformed before you—to His eternal glory, world without end. Amen.

—Eric Metaxas
New York City

INTRODUCTION

I REMEMBER THAT NIGHT as if it happened yesterday.

On June 8, 2003, at a Sunday evening service at Times Square Church, the Lord gave me a message of hope for a society that is at best confused, powerless, judgmental, and without faith in God: the message from the Gospel of Mark 9:14–29.

I was approached by many in our church on just how the Lord used this biblical passage and how it encouraged them both in their walk *and* in how to have a lasting impact in their homes, neighborhoods, communities, and state.

Almost fifteen years have passed since I delivered that particular message to my church. But that one message turned into a mission to encourage believers at large about the need for and the power of *prayer*. And from that one message a regional and then national radio ministry called It's Time to Pray was born!

Now that specific sermon has given birth to a larger message, which is contained in this book. I have thought for quite some time about the passage in Mark 9—I've looked at it, studied it, and read it over and over. The Lord has expanded the original message He gave me to show me just how impacting *prayer* can be in every area of both our personal lives and our community life.

The story in Mark 9 describes a journey most Christians will travel in their lifetime. It certainly reflects my life and my journey. I believe that the truth that is clearly annunciated by the Lord in Mark 9 is a critical message that the church needs to hear today.

There are far too many Christians who are walking around dejected, depressed, hopeless, powerless, and in bondage to the flesh. Friend, this is *not* what the Christian life is or should be. Jesus Christ fulfilled the will of the Father, and together they made a new covenant—one that set us free from the enslavement of sin and gave us new life both here and in eternity. Through the shed blood of Christ on the cross and His resurrection, Jesus restored our relationship with the living God and enabled us to live an abundant life!

Please understand, I'm not saying that as Christians we should never have a problem, feel down, or face trials. On the contrary, we will indeed face difficulty in life and experience spiritual warfare when living according to the Spirit rather than our flesh. But in the midst of these things, as believers we are not powerless and without hope. We are not under the power of our flesh or Satan anymore. Our power and hope are in God, and the Holy Spirit empowers us to live above the fray! The most powerful thing we can do in our lives is pray! The Bible tells us to pray without ceasing and to pray about everything.

If you are struggling in your walk—if you have failed yet again—if you look at the world around you and feel dejected, look up, for your redemption is nigh!

Join me in this book as we look at the tremendous lesson

Jesus gives us in Mark 9—along with some of my own personal experiences—and how it relates to us, our walk with God, and our impact on the world. You will find, as I have, that *it's time to pray*!

Chapter One

PRAYING FOR SALVATION

I HEAR IT ALL the time.

"Is there hope for my future? Is there a way out of my dilemma? Is there a way to change? Will my life ever be what it is supposed to be?" The ages...the gender...the season of life might all be different, but the questions remain the same.

Maybe you have asked these same questions. And maybe, just maybe, you don't like the answers that fill your mind... "I don't like what I am. I don't like what I do. I don't like how I act. I don't like what I've become.

"But I'm powerless to change."

GLORY TO GLORY

People are often drawn to power. Since the beginning of time mankind has fought to have power over others. Religious leaders have not been exempt from this desire to have authority over people. During the time of Jesus' ministry on earth, the religious leaders of the day—the Pharisees and the Sadducees— enjoyed a certain amount of power over the Jewish people by bargaining with the Roman officials. However, the power they held did nothing to *help* the people. Instead, it damaged their understanding of God and His purpose for them!

When Jesus began His public ministry, the Jewish people saw a difference in Him—He was not like the religious leaders who put heavy burdens on them. His teaching was powerful—piercing their hearts and minds. Mark 1:21–22 (NIV) says, "They went to Capernaum, and when the Sabbath came, Jesus went into the synagogue and began to teach. The people were amazed at his teaching, because he taught them as one who had authority, not as the teachers of the law."

What was this power that Jesus displayed? Was it the kind of power that did the impossible? Did Jesus' power bring about God's goodness, grace, and mercy in the people and situations that He touched? The answer, of course, is a resounding *yes*! Jesus taught with authority because He was and is *the authority*—and through this authority His power is displayed to show God's glory.

In the ninth chapter of the Gospel of Mark are two stories that display the authority and power of Jesus in an incredible way.

Mark 9:2–8 says:

> Now after six days Jesus took Peter, James, and John, and led them up on a high mountain apart by themselves; and He was transfigured before them. His clothes became shining, exceedingly white, like snow, such as no launderer on earth can whiten them. And Elijah appeared to them with Moses, and they were talking with Jesus. Then Peter answered and said to Jesus, "Rabbi, it is good for us to be here; and let us make three tabernacles: one for You, one for Moses, and one for Elijah"—because he did not know what to say, for they were greatly afraid. And a cloud came and overshadowed them; and a voice came

out of the cloud, saying, "This is My beloved Son. Hear Him!" Suddenly, when they had looked around, they saw no one anymore, but only Jesus with themselves.

Jesus had been on a mountain, and on that mountain He was transfigured—the glory of God that was in Him showed forth, and the disciples were in awe as they looked on. All of a sudden Moses and Elijah appeared with Jesus on that mountain and spoke with Him about His coming death in Jerusalem and the victory of salvation that would be won through Him for all people.

It was a mountaintop experience—a blessed spiritual victory filled with God's glory, revealing what He was able and going to do in the lives of His people!

I can just picture the disciples. They must have been overjoyed and feeling on top of the world because of what they had just witnessed. Their hopes were high, their faith was budding, and they must have felt as if everything was right with the world! I wonder if they even felt invincible. After all, they had just witnessed a great display of God's power—through the transfiguration of Jesus; the appearance of huge heroes of the faith, Moses and Elijah, who, of course, had been dead for generations but were now right in front of them and very much alive; and, of course, the voice of God telling them that Jesus was His Son and they were to listen to Him!

It was a great moment. It was an intense spiritual high.

But then they came down from the mountain, and as is the case so often in our lives, they were immediately met by the reality of a sinful, fallen world.

━◈━

Jos, Nigeria, 2003

I climbed the steps to the platform, constructed on the roof of a concession stand overlooking multiple soccer fields. The night sky above my head was clear, and the stars shone brightly. To the left of the platform, towering above us, was a huge video wall. There was another to our right. As I looked out over the sea of Nigerian faces, I could not see the edge of the crowd in any direction.

Local evangelical rally organizers estimated the mass of humanity that night at more than half a million men, women, and children. Standing on the platform, facing the multitude, I recalled the vivid warning I had received before leaving New York. When well-meaning brothers and sisters in Christ called into account the danger of our outreach in Nigeria, I simply asked, "Is the Christian life about preserving ourselves, or is it about obeying God and doing what He asks us to do?"

As I looked at the sea of humanity, I cued our praise band, and as it and the choir struck their first note, a tremendous wind suddenly hit the stage. Lightning flashed around us, and above our heads torrents of rain came at us from all four directions at once.

A large partition behind the choir risers came crashing down in the wind and injured several people. I felt in my gut that this was all demonic. All our electrical power was knocked out except for the podium microphone. I turned and saw the havoc that was happening in the choir and the fear that was sweeping over the platform as the wind, rain, and lightning continued under a clear, starry night sky.

Our entire team did the most important thing that we could ever do—we prayed.

There was no doubt that we were engaged in a spiritual struggle with the powers of darkness, but as we prayed, within moments we began to jump up and down on the platform, sensing the powerful presence of God beginning to come over us. As the storm raged, I asked Michael, an American missionary our church supported, to step up to the one working microphone and rebuke the storm. He did as I asked.

"In the name of Christ Jesus," Michael cried out, "wind and rain, stop!"

The moment Michael shouted those words, the wind, rain, and lightning stopped as suddenly as they had begun. I signaled to Harry, our praise band drummer, to begin beating out the rhythm to the traditional African praise song we had rehearsed.

The local Christian leaders had seen this kind of spiritual battle before. They were familiar with demonic forces of darkness. I was told a witch came into the crowd not far from the platform where I was to speak and began to curse the people who had come to worship. Yet rather than succumb to fear, the believers cried out to God. God, I am told, responded by paralyzing the witch where she stood and striking her dumb. Still in an attitude of prayer, the believers around her then led her to Christ.

After preaching a message of pure salvation—from Genesis to Revelation—to the crowd for over an hour, I issued a challenge to the throngs of people who had gathered: "If you want to have forgiveness for your sins, eternal life, and the life that God promises here on this earth through His Son—if you are serious about this— simply raise your hand."

The challenge of saving not just souls but lives in a crowd as large as the crowd outside of Jos, Nigeria, was overwhelming, especially with evil, opposing forces intent on doing harm in play.

But God is able to do the impossible through the prayers of His people.

No fewer than one hundred thousand people raised their hands to receive Christ as their Savior that night. With their hands still stretched skyward, I led them in a prayer to receive Jesus into their hearts.

Back in my hotel room hours later, I got on my knees to thank the Lord for what He had done. I had barely begun to pray when I heard the Lord say, "Don't limit Me. Don't limit what I can do."

———◆———

After the mountaintop experience of the transfiguration, Jesus came down the mountain and was immediately met by a man who was in trouble.

I often have to gently let new believers know that they may be floating on clouds and feeling on top of the world, only to get home and be assailed by unwanted thoughts or doubts about their salvation. Many times when we have enjoyed a tremendous spiritual victory, Satan is just around the corner, waiting to confront us. You go on a wonderful Christian retreat and experience the movement of the Holy Spirit, only to come home to a problem or a disaster. You hear a wonderful sermon that encourages you and lifts you to heavenly heights, only to be assailed by doubts on the drive home.

Jesus came down the mountain and was met not only by a troubled father but by the demons of hell.

The troubled father came to Him and said, "Teacher, I brought You my son, who has a mute spirit. And wherever it seizes him, it throws him down; he foams at the mouth, gnashes his teeth, and becomes rigid. So I spoke to Your disciples, that they should cast it out, but they could not." (Mark 9:17–18).

The boy was unable to hear things, and he was unable to speak. He was out of control and in agony. It had obviously been a long road for this man, his son, and his family, and there seemed to be no future for them. They were living in a situation that by human standards was hopeless. No one had been able to help, not even the disciples who had just experienced the glory of God on the mountain!

It's a situation that some of us face, and we say, "Is this the way it's always going to be? Is this my future?" We look at the trouble we face or the things that seem to bind us, and we sigh and say, "Well, my grandfather was this way, my father was this way, so I'm this way." Yet in our hearts we are aching to be different and to be set free. We look in the mirror and whisper, "Is there any chance that any of this can change? Does it have to be this way?"

Jesus responded to the man's declaration, saying, "O faithless generation, how long shall I be with you? How long shall I bear with you? Bring him to Me" (Mark 9:19).

When you first read this verse, you assume Jesus is talking to the father. However, He could be addressing the disciples or the religious leaders who were in the crowd as well. Jesus' statement can very well be directed to *all* of them. They had all failed to help the father and his son.

There's a type of religion in the world that has no bearing on what God is able to do. It can talk about God, just as the disciples at the bottom of the mountain could do, but without faith and the power of God, it cannot make a difference in somebody's life.

Some of you have had exposure to religion. You have tried to pray. You have gone to church services. However, what you have seen, heard, and experienced has not been something that really represents the transforming power that is available to every person who turns to Jesus Christ. The sad reality is that you can have religion, but if you don't have a relationship with Jesus Christ, it will get you nowhere!

When we know Jesus personally—when we have accepted Him into our hearts and minds as our Lord and Savior—we find that prayer is our lifeline; it's our method of communication and our vehicle to hear from God as well. Prayer, combined with the Word of God, is what draws us close to the Lord and builds our faith. If we ignore prayer, we will find our relationship with Christ subpar—a weakened and listless faith that does not bear fruit or transform the world around us.

I was instantly reminded of 1978, the year I first came to Christ. I was a young cop in Ottawa, Canada, only three years on the force. I had no public-speaking skills or training. I had certainly never preached a sermon. I was terrified of crowds and had struggled to even

speak out in the classroom throughout my youth—
afraid that I would be judged, criticized, or laughed at.
Nevertheless, as I walked my beat one day, I prayed,
"Lord Jesus, I want to win one hundred thousand
people to You before I die."

Twenty-five years later, in the fields outside Jos,
Nigeria, God answered my prayer in an instant. I hit
my knees beside the bed that night in 2003, astounded
that God would answer my prayer in such a majestic
way. But I was also astounded at what He then said.

"Don't limit Me," I heard God say again. "Don't
put boundaries around what I can do." After more
years of Bible study, prayer, and reflection, I realized
that the greatest sin of Israel was not in the building
of the golden calf at the foot of Mount Sinai. As vile a
sin as that was, the psalms teach us that the children
of Israel sinned even more when they limited the Holy
One of Israel by asking, "Can God furnish a table in
the wilderness?" (Ps. 78:19, KJV).

One of the greatest sins any one of us will ever
commit against God is suggesting that He has no right
or power to be God in our lives—or believing that
our lives have become such a wilderness that there
is no chance God could ever prepare a table before
us or use us to fulfill His mighty plan. I have confidence that God can and God will do what He tells us
through Scripture He can and will do, if we simply
pray and believe.

❖

The father and ailing, demon-possessed son had exhausted philosophies, ideas, and even religion to change the dire situation they were in. Though tired from trying to get help and weary from failing in all his attempts to fix his son's problem, the worn-out father found some hope in this extraordinary "man" from Galilee and said to Jesus, "If You can do anything, have compassion on us and help us" (Mark 9:22).

Like this dear father, some of you are not overly filled with faith that your situation can change. You have a glimmer of hope in your heart that Jesus can fix your problem, and your prayer is exactly like this father's: "If You can do anything, Jesus; if You are still listening; if You are more than what people have told me You are; if You are beyond what I have seen in the people who are supposed to represent You—if You can do anything, Jesus, would You have mercy on me and save me?"

Have you cried out to God? Be intentional in your prayer—ask God to intervene in your life and in your situation. Everything Jesus did was intentional. He didn't do anything randomly; everything He said and everything He did fulfilled the purpose that God had laid out before the foundation of the world: the salvation of mankind.

———◆◆◆———

I remember sitting in a church in my very early twenties, when I had just come to Jesus Christ as my Lord and Savior, and I remember hearing an evangelist preach on the verse "All things are possible to him that believes!" (Mark 9:23, DARBY). It was the first time I'd ever heard it in my whole life. In fact, before hearing this truth, my life had been defined by what people said I could or couldn't do, or what I was able to become or not able to become. I started to believe that God could take my life and do something supernatural through it if I prayed and believed.

What God taught me and reminded me of that night in Jos, Nigeria, in 2003 is that there should be no limit to my belief if my belief is in Him. I am human, and, like anyone else, I can believe too small if I only think in human dimensions, if my thoughts are confined to the natural.

But the prayer of a young Canadian cop in 1978 went on and got more specific. "I don't want these one hundred thousand people to only make a public profession of faith," I prayed. "But I want them to actually walk with You, Lord, and end up one day at the foot of Your throne." As I prayed that prayer, I felt in my heart as if I was not speaking into the wind. I felt as if God not only heard me but would take delight in doing what to me would be impossible.

How a kid born in Rouyn-Noranda, a rural copper-mining town in northwest Quebec (population forty thousand), came to pray such prayers and welcome such multitudes into the kingdom of God is a mystery to anyone but God.

———✦———

I've watched over the years how some people jump at the gift of salvation in Christ, while others struggle with making a decision to follow Jesus.

Many people are caught between two belief systems. If I were to ask you, "Do you believe all things are possible with God?" you would probably look me in the eye—whether or not you're walking with God or whether or not your sins are forgiven—and say, "I believe that!"

The problem is that you also believe something else. You believe that your life is defined by certain borders, by certain limitations, by certain bondages, or by your life experience—whether it's education, culture, the environment, or what others have said to you over the years.

Yes, you believe that with God all things are possible, but you also believe what your life has become through the various influences that have defined who you are in the world.

Lord, I believe, but help my unbelief.

Rid your life of the boundaries and definitions that were given to you by others and by your culture. As a believer, you are a new creation in Christ, and you are who God says you are! You are loved, and you are accepted by Jesus Christ. He has given you a calling and a divine purpose in life, and He has given you the Holy Spirit to be able to live out your walk on a daily basis.

Do you need more faith? Friend, it's time to give yourself fully to God in prayer.

The Bible tells us, in James 1:5–7, "If any of you lacks wisdom, let him ask of God, who gives to all liberally and without reproach, and it will be given to him. But let him ask in faith, with no doubting, for he who doubts is like a wave of the sea driven and tossed by the wind."

The Lord wants us to be intentional in our prayers. Be specific; be direct; pray according to God's will, and take Him at His word!

God always answers the prayers of His people. The answer

may be delayed; the answer may be "no," "yes," or "not yet," but there will be an answer. Keep praying and keep believing— God is able to do far above what you would ever expect.

———◆———

I had the privilege of leading my father to Christ in his last hour of consciousness. It was December 2002. My father was eighty-one years old, and he was battling colon cancer and underwent a bowel resection, resulting in a colostomy. Because of the type of cancer he had, the feces inside his colostomy bag was especially foul. The stench was intolerable. The nurses who came to change the bag wore masks and plastic gloves. During my previous visit, the bag needed to be emptied, and, rather than wait for a nurse to visit, I did it.

As a former cop, I had seen my share of blood and guts and smelled a lot of things I would rather not have smelled. But that bag was nothing like anything I had ever experienced. Yet changing that colostomy bag seemed like the kind of thing that Jesus would do out of love. God might have given me that opportunity to demonstrate for my father the value Jesus placed on serving others in love—especially when the service was costly, taxing, or unpleasant. Without the benefit of a mask or gloves, I removed the bag and attached another after cleaning the area around the colostomy.

In the grand scheme of things, my gesture meant very little. The bag had been replaced many times before, and after I left, it would be changed again. Although it wasn't necessarily my place to do such a thing, it was just a way that I could help my father live in a slightly more dignified way in that moment and demonstrate to him and to my family that love doesn't hesitate to get its hands dirty. Jesus' love went far beyond dirty hands—all the way to nail-pierced hands.

Anything I could do in His name was insignificant compared with His ultimate sacrifice. Yet small acts can sometimes be the modeling of godly love that non-believers can grasp.

I had been back and forth from New York to Rouyn-Noranda several times as my father's condition worsened. I had gently, but firmly, persisted with my desire to lead him to the Lord, and he had politely waved me off, saying, "That's OK for you, Carter, not for me."

During the second-to-last trip I made to Rouyn-Noranda to check on my father, the trip when I changed his colostomy bag, he began listening to my witnessing with more interest. Somehow he was beginning to move beyond the completely practical to consider the far less practical things of faith. He had also begun praying. This was a remarkable softening for a man who had been angry with me ever since I became a Christian and resigned from the police force.

A few weeks before my final trip to see my father, my senior pastor at Times Square Church, David Wilkerson, said to me, "God is going to give you a window with your father."

I felt a sense of urgency as I left New York to fly to Rouyn-Noranda, not knowing that it would be the last time that I would see my dad alive. David Wilkerson's words were fresh in my mind as the flight to Canada lifted off from LaGuardia. The plan was for me to go to my mother's house, shower, and have dinner with her before going to the hospital. As soon as I arrived at my mother's house, the phone rang.

It was my brother. My brother and I were not on much warmer terms than I had been on with my father since I joined the ministry. So his phone call, asking for me, struck me as odd.

"Dad and I are waiting for you," he said.

My brother's words struck me as extremely odd. I wondered if God was calling me to my father's bedside and the urgency I sensed before leaving New York was real. Had the Lord been that spot-on with the message He delivered to me through David Wilkerson? I told my mom I would be back for dinner and we could go to the hospital together later that evening.

When I arrived at the hospital, my father was seated in a chair next to the door of his room. My brother, Shawn, was standing against the wall beyond the chair.

"Hi, Dad," I said. "Have you been praying?"

"I've been praying all week."

"Are you ready to pray with me?" I asked.

"If you would like that," he said, "I would like to do that."

It was a precious moment that I will never forget. I knew that he knew what he was agreeing to. We had covered that territory on my prior visits, especially the visit just prior, when I wasn't sure if I would see him again. My father was very aware of the profound commitment he was about to make. As I sat and we prayed together, we picked up the conversation right where we left off on my prior visit, when he had allowed me to explain what it means to be a Christian.

I led him in a prayer of surrender that must have lasted over five minutes. I led him around Mount Sinai and through the wilderness. I didn't want to leave anything out. I wanted him to know—truly understand—what this meant. As I would do with the crowd in Jos, Nigeria, the following year, I prayed with him from Genesis to Revelation.

We prayed in great detail. I didn't want him to go through the motions to appease me, and I didn't want him to be the least bit confused. "Jesus, I need You as my Savior," we prayed. "I open my heart....I give You my life....Jesus, I receive You as my Lord and Savior."

Everything I would do during an altar call at Times Square Church I did with my father in his Rouyn-Noranda hospital room. After we had prayed through, I helped him stand up and put him in bed. Shawn was still leaning against the wall, literally frozen in disbelief. To know my father, you knew he wouldn't have prayed that prayer if he didn't mean it. His word had always been his bond. He was a man of truth. I never in my life heard him tell a lie. I never heard him embellish anything. Whatever he said, he said straight out. It was what it was.

Once he was settled in bed, I touched my father's arm gently.

"I love you, Dad."

"Carter, I love you."

Shawn's amazement only increased. This talk of love was astonishing for my father, who had never *been one to speak so openly about emotions, especially an emotion as intimate as love.*

But God spoke through my father that evening in a way that couldn't have made His life-transforming power more evident. Once he was in bed, Dad and I talked for the next hour about heaven and freedom from sin. As I prepared to leave and return to my mom's house, I said, "Dad, it will be so awesome when I get to heaven to see you there."

"Carter, I'll be there."

He wasn't joking.

For twenty-four years my father had been angry that I became a Christian and did not follow the family plan to become a lawyer. Despite all of that, I simply believed that God would answer my prayers for my father's salvation. I never wavered in my believing— even when it looked impossible, I continued to believe.

Now, as my father lay in the hospital dying, God brought my dad to Himself. I left the hospital, promising to return after having dinner with Mom. When we did return, my dad had slipped into a coma, and shortly after, he passed into glory.

…And a twenty-four-year journey came to a marvelous end.

DELAY IS NOT DEFEAT

Second Peter 3:9 says, "The Lord is not slack concerning His promise, as some count slackness, but is longsuffering toward us, not willing that any should perish but that all should come to repentance."

Patiently waiting for God's answer is not always something we like to do. I'm afraid that many believers, especially American Christians, want instant answers. Our flesh, like the culture around us, wants instant gratification. However, God often works in our lives through the process of *delay*. Let's put it this way: if it is better for us to receive an instant (or quick) answer to our prayer, God will certainly give it. Yet we need to understand that "better for us" does not necessarily mean physically beneficial to us as much as spiritually beneficial.

The Lord is always interested in maturing us in our faith—bringing about things in our lives that groom us to be more like Jesus. So if an answer to prayer is immediate, it is for our benefit. In the same way, we need to understand that God often delays the answer to our prayers to benefit us spiritually and physically, and for the Lord's greater glory.

Jesus was dealing with many different scenarios in this account of the father and his possessed son. First, He had three of His disciples (who had witnessed His transfiguration on the mount) in the middle of all the chaos and confusion of the moment. Second, He had the discontented crowd of people questioning the other disciples as to their lack of power to heal the boy. Third, He had the disciples who were confused as to why God didn't answer their prayer and heal the child. And finally He had the father of the child who was exhausted and desperate to find help for his beloved son.

God's delay in answering prayer affected everyone in this story. Yet what we need to understand is that when God delays in answering prayer, we can be sure He is working in the hearts of *all* the people affected by the situation!

When I think of Jos, Nigeria, and the attack of the enemy

that we had to face, I want you to know that the Lord had taken years before this exercising my faith in order for me to not be deterred at that moment on the stage. I was only able to stand firm against the spiritual attack on our team in Jos because the Lord had "trained" me for many years on just how to do that! Faith does not develop overnight, nor does it grow by a life of ease.

Then in the situation of my father, I had to wait until God had worked in his heart before I could lead him in prayer. In fact, I had to wait until my testimony as a believer could help my father's resistance subside in order for him to receive Christ.

The Lord has taught me about trust and faith in all the delays in my life!

Let me ask you, Are you experiencing a delay to your prayer right now? Is there someone you have been praying for to be saved—perhaps even over many years—who still has not come to know the Lord? Please don't be discouraged. And whatever you do, don't give up! In order for faith to grow, it has to be tried and tested before you see God deliver and bring about His salvation. Another way God uses delays is so others can observe your walk with the Lord over time. One of the greatest witnesses for Christ is when people see how a believer responds to a difficulty in his or her life! If they see you patiently waiting on God—filled with peace as you endure a trial—it helps them see that what you have in Christ is real!

God uses delays to bring us to the point where our trust is solely in Him. Perhaps the disciples were boasting that they could deliver this child (especially since they had witnessed the glory of the transfiguration) not because of their faith but because of the presumption that they were able to do what Jesus could do. We all have the tendency to be impetuous, especially when it comes to wanting to see our loved ones saved and serving the Lord. But it is by faith and patience the kingdom of God is established. Lamentations 3:24–26 (NIV) says, "I say to myself, 'The LORD is my portion; therefore I will wait for him.' The LORD is good to those whose hope is in him, to the one who seeks him; it is good to wait quietly for the salvation of the LORD."

JESUS ANSWERS THE FATHER'S PRAYER

When the father of the child cried out to Jesus, the Lord responded to his measure of faith and said, "'Deaf and dumb spirit, I command you, come out of him and enter him no more!' Then the spirit cried out, convulsed him greatly, and came out of him. And he became as one dead, so that many said, 'He is dead.' But Jesus took him by the hand and lifted him up, and he arose" (Mark 9:25–27).

The devil had a comfortable place in this boy's life. The young man was in bondage to sin, his flesh, and the enemy. But through his father's prayer and measure of faith, Jesus was called to do what no one else had been able to do—set this young man free.

The Bible tells us that "if the Son makes you free, you shall be free indeed" (John 8:36).

Sometimes it's all you and I can do to lay flat on our backs, raise one hand, and pray, "Jesus Christ, Son of God, this is all I have."

And Jesus says, "That's all I need!"

Jesus answered the prayer of a father who believed, even in small measure, that He could do what no one else had been able to do—set his son and his family free. It seems too good to be true, doesn't it? There is no formula or ritual or positive thinking; it's simply a matter of prayer (crying out to God) and a willingness to believe that God is who He said He is!

With God nothing is impossible.

I heard a well-intentioned person say one day, "Don't give up on that person—God can save them!" They are right in that God can save *anyone* and we should always keep on praying for the salvation of our friends, coworkers, family, and those we know. But the one thing I would change about that statement is that it is not an issue of giving up on that person; it is an issue of continuing to believe and trust God. We should never give up on what God wants to do in our lives or in others!

I've heard many, many stories of how people have prayed for years for the salvation of a loved one. How can one do this without getting discouraged? When we truly know the One we are praying to, we know our efforts are not in vain! "Huge happenings are not always visible to the naked eye—especially in the spiritual realm....Sometimes we pray and pray and seemingly see no change in the situation. But that's only true from our perspective. If we could see from heaven's standpoint, we would know all that God is doing and intending to do in our lives. We would see God working in hearts in ways we cannot know. We would see God orchestrating circumstances that we know nothing about. We would see a galaxy of details being set in place for the moment when God brings the answer to fulfillment."[1]

God answered a specific prayer I prayed when I was a new believer—to see one hundred thousand people come to salvation—many years later in my life. He delayed the answer to that prayer so He could test and grow my faith; that way it was not about what Carter Conlon could do but all about what God could do!

We all have family, friends, and relatives somewhere who need our prayers. *Become intentional*—fast and ask the Lord to place one individual on your heart and begin praying for him or her. Don't get discouraged if it takes time to see an answer to your prayer! Our job is to bring people to Jesus in prayer and to leave the manner by which our prayer is answered to God alone.

———◆◆———

Christmas Day hadn't yet arrived when my dad came to Christ. Nevertheless, in the snowy December evening as I left the hospital, I was singing, "Hallelujah," clapping my hands, crying, laughing, skipping, jumping, and praising the Lord. Anyone who saw me would have thought I was under the influence of something potent or that I had simply lost my mind.

I was out of my mind with joy, rejoicing, along with the host of heaven, that my father had finally found the way to his eternal home.

My father's coming to Christ was like a mighty oak falling in the forest. No one could have moved him except for God Himself. But in his final hour of consciousness, he had accepted Christ Jesus as his Lord and Savior. I have often wondered if the Lord put him to sleep so soon after his salvation to keep him from doubting and changing his mind. Regardless I know my father is waiting for me in heaven.

"Carter, I'll be there," were the last words he spoke to me.

Yes, Dad, we will meet again, and we will rejoice!

———◆◆———

Important Takeaways From This Chapter

Key thought: When praying (and believing) for salvation, be intentional.

Key word: Salvation—In the Greek language the word is *sozo*, which means to keep safe; to rescue; to heal; to deliver; to preserve; and, of course, to offer eternal life.

Key insight: In Mark 9 praying for salvation included:

- In the case of the child, deliverance from demonic power

- In the case of my father, spiritual salvation

- In the case of the Jos, Nigeria, crusade, the supernatural cessation of an attack by the enemy using natural forces against the meeting, and also spiritual salvation

Chapter Two

PRAYING FOR LIFE

I READ RECENTLY ABOUT a town outside of San Francisco that has a population of five hundred. Interestingly enough, this small town is surrounded by cemeteries with thousands of graves. There are literally far more people who are dead than alive in this town. It's no wonder that the entrance to the town displays a sign that says "It's great to be alive!"

When I look around at our society, I can say without hesitation that there are far more people who are barely living than who believe that "it's great to be alive."

Jesus said, "The thief does not come except to steal, and to kill, and to destroy. *I have come that they may have life, and that they may have it more abundantly*" (John 10:10, emphasis added).

Are you living the abundant life that Christ promised, or do you merely exist?

I've experienced the *barely living* side of life...

My official job was bartender. My equally official, but more undercover, job was bouncer. My intimate familiarity with alcohol and my willingness to fight at the drop of a hat, on or off the hockey rink, made me ideally suited for the combined responsibilities.

Guys were mobbing the bar, trying to drink up enough courage to ask women to dance. My hands were full. Except for that moment when I looked up and saw Teresa standing in the doorway, I was hustling and bustling trying to fill drink orders. After she and the girlfriend she was with disappeared into the crowd, all I saw were mostly guys crowding the bar.

It was ironic that I wound up as the bartender/ bouncer, despite my qualifications. I had actually applied to be a residence fellow, which is a dorm greeter. The job entailed orienting new residents in the dorm, answering questions, showing them where things were, and adjudicating if there were problems between residents throughout the year. I went to the orientation session and listened intently. I was still struggling with fear and very afraid that someone would single me out, so I didn't speak up or participate much.

At the end of the orientation, I was shocked that the leader came up to me, thanked me for coming, and told me that I wasn't "leadership material," as far as he was concerned. That was the end of my career as a residence fellow—a career that never got started.

Bartending/bouncing was something I apparently was "material" for. Looking back, years later, at the rejection, I realized that if we are obsessed with what other people think of us, we will never become what God wants us to be.

<hr>

It's sad to say, but many Christians live their lives in the wilderness because they came to the conclusion that God could not do what He said He could do.

I bring this up again because all people who know Christ will come to that crossroads at least once and probably more often during their lifetimes. We're never stationary. We can't stand still in Christ. We either move forward or backward. Do we trust God to do what He has promised to do, or do we hang back in our own doubt and insecurity?

There is a time after we're saved that we read the promises of God and sail right to the shore of a new life. It's clear that all we need to do is step out of the boat onto dry land. All we need to do is start walking, and God will make the promises real. Yet many people can't make a break from words that were previously spoken over their lives, so they go backward and live their entire Christian existence in a wilderness.

In their wilderness they are always searching for joy, but it constantly eludes them. They search for meaning, but everything they come up with is empty. They look for direction, but all they can see is more desert. If you can imagine the children of Israel in that wilderness, it was a never-ending succession of funerals. There was an absence of life and an absence of joy. All the wine of life was gone.

I know it wasn't the courtship that Teresa wanted or deserved. Nevertheless, our life together had begun.

It was supposed to be what I wanted. Yet instead of feeling elated, the wound within my heart remained open, and the seeping misery mingled with a hundred other wounds from my lifetime up to that point. I didn't fully trust that Teresa wasn't going to have a change of heart and decide that she really didn't love me after all. In reality, I couldn't possibly have been easy to love. With all that resentment and pain in my heart, I was not pleasant to be around. I guess I was just waiting for Teresa to figure that out.

My drinking got worse. I continued to ride out panic attacks with Valium and whiskey. My temper was as bad as ever, and I lashed out at people with little or no provocation. I testify to this day about how much suffering I caused Teresa and our young children in those early years. Even after I was saved and the Lord cured my panic attacks, my anger was slow to subside. Teresa cried a lot. I embarrassed her on many occasions by simply being callous to the feelings of others.

Teresa was horrified. She was trapped with an angry man who couldn't behave himself. She was a brilliant student who aspired at one point to be a lawyer. She had all the bells and whistles to do it and would have done it if she hadn't become so invested in saving me from myself. I dragged her down. I was her albatross. But she truly kept looking to God to help. When I was still into booze and anger, she was trying to invoke the almighty God.

UNBELIEF IS AT THE ROOT OF POWERLESSNESS

Mark 9:17 says, "I have brought unto thee my son" (KJV).

Going back to the wonderful lessons found in the ninth chapter of the Gospel of Mark, I want to call particular attention to verse 17. Jesus was about to take the father of the child on a quick spiritual journey from unbelief to faith in Him. In many ways this child, whom the father dearly loved, had been possessed by demonic power that denied him the privilege of living a full and robust life. He was alive physically but dead to true living. Demonic power was inwardly tearing him apart, and physically he was constantly in harm's way every time the evil spirit put him into the fire and the water. The boy could not say, "It's great to be alive."

The situation was dire. No one had been able to help this father and his son. Even the religious leaders and Jesus' disciples failed to offer relief due to their lack of faith. Even though the religious leaders had the Old Testament writings, and the disciples the very words of Christ, none of these leaders took the teaching to heart. Their unbelief was on public display. When speaking to Jesus, the father clearly pointed the finger of blame to the disciples' inability to help, never considering his own bankrupt faith caused by unbelief. Jesus knew that unbelief was widespread throughout the crowd. Yet His first job was to show the father his own unbelieving heart. Jesus was poised to take the father on a journey to reveal his own spiritual depravity and need before delivering his son from Satan's grip.

I wish now, for those who answer altar calls, that change would come as fast as salvation. But it doesn't. It certainly didn't for me or for Teresa. Once saved, you will be changed. That's God's promise. If you claim to believe and don't change, you're a hypocrite. But even for those who change, the change can be excruciatingly slow.

Even after I was saved, I was a workaholic and was almost never home. And when I was, I am sure Teresa wished I wasn't. She was a young mother with a small boy, stuck in the boondocks. A bright student, she could have been devouring legal journals nightly and advancing swiftly with her nearly photographic memory and tremendous comprehension of complex scholarly concepts.

Given what I caused Teresa to endure, especially in the early years of our marriage, our ministries—separately and corporately—are a great testimony to God's ability to work all things together for good. Even though I was a changed man the moment my feet hit the floor on May 13, 1978, I was a long, long way from where Christ wanted me to be. I'm happy to say that by God's amazing grace (and Teresa's long-suffering) the Lord transformed my life.

Perhaps the deepest grief in my life, a grief that almost swallowed me for a season, was my regret over how I had treated my wife. It has given me a heart for the people who answer altar calls. I know how sin will find an expression in the body. I know how flesh will war against spirit. I know how transformation can be agonizingly slow. I know how God set me free from fear in an instant but took years to take away my anger.

I know how, even after the sword cuts the roots, a dead tree can stand for years. My temper took eight years to control following my salvation. I had God's promise that I would change and that my life would change. But without an understanding of grace, I set about to try and force the change to happen faster than God had planned. Imagine the suffering that caused Teresa and my children. In Mark 11:12–25 Jesus cursed the fig tree, and His disciples saw it standing the next morning. It was withered, but it was still standing. I remained withered for many years, even though I had the Word of God in my heart.

Some Christians are just miserable. They go to church, and they become critical of anything that doesn't move them. The worship, the music, the preaching…none of it satisfies them. But the reality is that they are not going anywhere in God. They are trying to propel their Christian life in the natural.

LOSE YOUR LIFE, AND YOU WILL GAIN IT

What is preventing us from living the abundant life that Christ promised us? The answer is as simple as it is difficult: *self.*

It's interesting that analysts often peg different decades with various labels. I remember the 1980s being called "the decade of *me*—it's all about *me*." Yet the reality is that every decade and every culture has exalted *self* over others and over God.

The abundant life that God promises is not based on venerating *self*. The wonderful life that Christ promises us is not about personal blessing, personal prosperity, or personal aggrandizement. This self-focus brings about spiritual defeat and immaturity as well as opening the door to immorality.

We cannot live the Christian life by our own mechanisms or power. When *self* propels our Christian walk, we fail.

WHEN UNBELIEF IS PRESENT, SELF WILL ALWAYS REIGN

Mark 9:18 says, "I spoke to Your disciples, that they should cast it out, but they could not."

The perception of the father was that it was somebody else's problem (and lack of power) as to why his son remained in bondage to demonic strongholds. Today in our culture we would term this condition a *victim mentality*—"My problems are always caused by other people, not me!"

The father wanted to make it clear to Jesus that his son was not healed because of the disciples' lack of power. In essence, he was saying, "I did my part, Jesus. I brought my son to Your so-called disciples, and they could do nothing for him." How many times have we heard this said by friends, family, or coworkers? They come to church—to try it out—and if God doesn't answer their prayers immediately or in the way they think He should, they declare that Christianity doesn't work and refuse to go back!

When a heart is hardened toward God, every crisis is because someone else has failed you.

We can all look over our shoulder and recount the many times others—including closest family members—have hurt us.

We all also have plenty of unmet expectations and disappointments stored up in our memories that we can use to shift the blame for our own problems.

In my own life, I could never match up to my father's expectations. No matter how hard I worked for him, it was never enough. I could very easily blame my anger and need of affirmation on him. When I was at college and applied to be a residence fellow or dorm greeter, I was told I could never become a leader—I had no leadership material in me. I could have easily said, "My struggles began with that one rejection."

None of us are exempt from being hurt or mistreated. Jesus, knowing the real problem was an untreated state of unbelief, said, "O faithless generation..."

The real problem was not the disciples' powerlessness (though Jesus would address this issue with the disciples as well) but the father's own lack of faith in God for deliverance.

This father could have dedicated himself over the years to the Word of God and to building up his faith, but he focused on his son's condition rather than on God's covenant promise to be a father to His people. When Jesus asked the father how long his son had dealt with this condition, it wasn't that He didn't already know, but He wanted the father to recognize the years he had wasted because of his own hardness of heart. The dear father was so focused on the problem instead of looking to God that it's easy to see how his heart became duller and harder to the things of God.

Jesus said, "For whoever desires to save his life will lose it, but whoever loses his life for My sake will find it" (Matt. 16:25).

When we come to the place where we die—die to our rights, our plans, our desires, and our way of thinking—we are then propelled by the life of Jesus living in us! The reason we lack abundant life, the reason we lack victory in our walk, the reason our prayers are stale and ineffective, the reason we have no joy is because we have not died to *self*—*self* is still on the throne instead of Christ. How do we die to self? How do we stop propelling our faith through our flesh? We realize that the gospel is about grace—it's about what God has done and not about what we can do!

———◆———

My season of Christianity based on works and human effort was heavy into being in the right place and doing the right things. I was intent on pressing my children into Christian service and not allowing them to make the kinds of bad decisions I had made. Being that tightfisted and legalistic with Christianity has a bounce-back effect. My children couldn't handle it because there was no joy in it.

To be clear, I was preaching a gospel of grace in those early years. How could I be a Christian and not know the Word and comprehend what it means? But mine was a message of grace coupled with human effort. I should say, heavy on the human effort. There was no joy in me. My attitude and the mandate I made for my family was that we were going to doggedly serve God.

I could never enjoy myself. If I went to a summer fair, I would feel weighted down by a burden to save people. "How can I enjoy myself," I would think, "while people all around me are lost and going to hell?"

My kids began to resent me. They loved me as their father, but they resented the life I was forcing them to lead. One day, when we were preparing to go to some social event or another, one of my children said, "Dad, please stay home. Everywhere we go, you just ruin it for us."

I can see so clearly now that my dogged Christianity was nauseating. If I had the chance to raise my children again, I would be outside playing ball with them more often. It would be a very different life for them. But I didn't come into a covenant understanding of the joy of the Lord until I was thirty-seven years old. I was saved at the age of twenty-four and wouldn't fully understand grace for thirteen years.

I was four years into full-time ministry, Jason was barely a teenager, Jared was knocking on the door of his teen years, and Kate had yet to celebrate her first decade on earth. I was driven to do what I was doing. As I said, there was no joy in me. I forced them to get up at 5:30 in the morning and do our devotions together because I felt that was what God wanted us to do.

The Christianity I forced on my family was utterly unattractive—well-intentioned, but foolish. It was stupid and immature and lacking in any true understanding of grace. I received full covenant when I broke down and couldn't do it anymore in my own strength. When that happened, I finally realized that I could only go forward by grace.

When we come to Christ, the blood of Jesus covers our sin, and we become the righteousness of God through Christ. But there is an outworking of that righteousness—and that work is done in and through us as we die to self and live for Christ.

If I am righteous, then I desire to live like a righteous man should. I am in Christ; Christ is in me. I've been cleansed of my sin; it no longer has dominion over my life. So by the power of God's Holy Spirit within me, I now want to live a life that looks like who I am in Christ.

We live out our righteousness by living in conformity to God's truth and purpose for our lives.

When we make the choice to live a right life according to the Word of God, we don't try to push the borders; we don't try to see how close we can get to the fire without being burned. We make the choice to see how close to the cross we can get in this life. We make the choice to walk in conformity.

When we're walking in right relationship with God, we become unstoppable on this earth.

None of what I'm saying applies to the game player. If you're a religious game player, you only come to church for fire insurance. You don't really want to live for God. Instead, you want to enjoy everything the world's got to offer through the week and then come to church on Sunday morning to get rid of your sense of guilt because you know in your heart you've done wrong. However, you have no intention of turning away from doing wrong; you just want to have the covering of church for salvation.

You will never experience the life that God has for you—the abundant life—until you let go of the world. Time and again in Scripture we see that when God's people embraced the pleasures of the culture that surrounded them, they lost their strength.

And when the theological focus of the house of God became about personal pleasure, personal prosperity, and self-elevating doctrines, it took away the life and strength of the church. It rendered us powerless!

Are you willing to die to self?

Are you willing to walk away from that which is weakening you? Are you willing to embrace that which will give you strength? Are you willing to live on this earth for the purposes of God?

Do you believe that God can put words in your mouth and courage in your heart that are not there today but that you are willing to have there? Do you believe that He can give you a passion for His kingdom, for His honor, for His glory? Do you believe that you can stand when confronted by darkness? Do you believe honestly that your life will make a difference?

If we have the heart of Christ beating within us, we can't live self-consumed lives. We will be ineffective, weak, and poor representatives of Christ. *Self* has to be dethroned so that God has His rightful place in your life. It's time to let go and die to self and put God on the throne!

One night after preaching, I couldn't sleep. A very strange feeling came over me, and I knew it wasn't from God. I'd start to drift off and suddenly feel as if I were falling off the end of the bed even though I wasn't. I returned home to my family and went out to play with my church hockey team. I loved playing hockey, but all of a sudden I couldn't keep my breath. I would play for a shift and come back to the bench gasping for breath. It was all very strange for me. I couldn't even play the next shift before I had to come back to the bench and catch my breath. I couldn't recuperate. I was a very fit thirty-seven-year-old man. I was in incredible physical condition. But I couldn't get my breath back, even after sitting.

When I went into church on Sunday to preach, my head felt as if it were splitting open. I was still short of breath, and I had no energy. Sunday after Sunday I tried, and the massive headaches continued. I couldn't raise my voice because the pain was excruciating. I went home after church on those days, took a fistful of Tylenol, and lay down. This went on for at least six months. It took me a long time to realize that I was having a physical breakdown.

Then, when I felt I couldn't take it anymore, I went out onto a country road, raised my arms, and threw my head back. "Is this how You reward those who serve You?" I screamed. "I gave You my job, my house; I put my family in Your hands. I've given You the best of all the strength that I have. And You respond by taking away my strength. Is there some kind of crooked side to You that I haven't seen? Do You get some kind of delight in doing this to Your servants?"

I was furious. If God had said to me in that moment, "I'm going to turn you to ashes," I would have said, "Go ahead."

In my heart I believed that I had given God everything that I had. "You gave me a vision, God," I ranted, "that I would see thousands, even hundreds of thousands, turn to You. So I went out to do that, and You respond by taking away my strength?" I shouted, complained, and railed against the Lord until it was all out. My tank was empty. I was spent. I knelt down on the road, broken and empty.

Then He spoke to me. I heard God say softly, "I love you." That wasn't what I expected. I expected a response in kind. But that wasn't God's plan. I melted at His words. It was what I had always longed for my earthly father to say, and now God Himself was saying it.

"What do You want me to do?" I exhaled.

"Carter," the Lord said to me, "I only want you to do what I ask you to do. You've done many, many things that I didn't ask you to do."

"I will do as You say, God."

As soon as I spoke those words, it was as if a thirteen-year burden was lifted from my shoulders. I recall one man in our church who was up and down, up and down, sober, drunk, sober, drunk. I used to grab him by the shirt and get in his face, saying, "I stopped drinking—you can stop drinking."

"But I can't," he would cry. "I can't."

"Of course you can," I would bellow at him.

About three weeks after God set me free from my own zealousness, a guy came up to me and said, "Pastor, I feel so much hope in your preaching these past few weeks."

He was sensing that I had turned my control and striving over to God. I wasn't in his face anymore because I had come to realize that it wasn't my strength that helped me stop drinking. It was God's strength. Being in his face would be the ultimate hypocrisy. I had come to the end of my own strength. I needed

God's strength in my life, and it had produced in me a joy and a song that I hadn't known.

——•——

If there ever was a time to intercede, if there ever was a time for you and me to say, "O God, O God, O God, would You help me die to self? God, would You lift me out of the luke-warm mediocrity that seems to have gripped this church age? Would You give me the grace to make a difference? Would You raise me up, O God, in whatever sphere of influence You give me, whatever place You take me to? Would You help me? Would You be my strength? Would You be my voice?" the time is now.

THE SPIRITUAL JOURNEY TO FAITH

Mark 9:22 says, "If You can do anything, have compassion on us and help us."

There was a slow progression of change that took place in the father's conversation with Jesus. At first there was only criticism toward the disciples for *their* lack of power; then after Jesus brings to his attention his own lack of faithfulness over the years, the father asks the divine healer if He could do anything. And then, for the first time, the father inserts the word *us*, recognizing that both he and his son needed God's healing!

The father finally understood that he was part of the problem and needed Christ's healing as much as his son did. This change reveals three distinct revelations taking place: his own lack of power and ability to effect any spiritual change, either in the boy's life or his own; his absolute need of compassion and grace due to his own negligence of prayer and the Word; and his request for help was the beginning of faith.

Jesus could now challenge the father with the words "If thou canst believe, all things are possible to him that believeth" (v. 23, KJV). Jesus had broken up the fallow ground of this man's heart and was now planting the seed of faith in fertile soil. Conviction of the Holy Spirit is always a win-win situation. Although it may be difficult to hear what God has to say about our heart condition, the end result always bears fruit!

When the father said to Jesus, "I believe; help my un-belief!" he acknowledged he believed what Jesus said while also seeing that his heart still held vestiges of unbelief (v. 24).

I wonder, Can you relate to this father?

Do you believe what Jesus says but also struggle with doubt in your heart?

I want you to be encouraged by something. Once the father recognized his need for Christ and asked for help with his unbelief, that was all Jesus needed to perform a miracle of deliverance and healing for the boy. The spiritual journey was complete—not only had the father received his son back whole and delivered, but he too was free from the grip of an unbelieving and hardened heart.

When God came and started to carry my cross, I was freed from what I thought was God's law but was, in fact, mostly my law. All of a sudden I no longer felt compelled to please God because I couldn't. I could stop trying to be a Christian in my own strength because it didn't work. I was at rest. I began living by God's promises to me, not by my promises to God.

The Lord came to give us life and life more abundantly. When we walk in grace and live our lives for Christ, we experience lives that are full of the fruit of the Spirit, and instead of living for ourselves, we live for God and others.

That's what the cross was ultimately about; it was for the benefit of others that Jesus went to that cross. So God, help me to represent You and to know the power of Christ within me so that Your kingdom may be advanced in my generation.

May I just give you a word of encouragement? Don't limit God! Don't tell Him what He can do with your life, and don't tell Him what He can't do. He's God; He can do whatever He wants to do. It's the yielded heart that gets the victory. It's the person who decides to go with God who finds the incredible favor of the Lord.

***

There is a measure in all of us that will try to "be Christian" instead of allowing God to bring us to Himself. We read that virtue is a Christian characteristic. So we resolve to be virtuous, and we're completely sincere—speaking the truth at all times and doing the "right" things. But our best intentions are still human. Our best intentions always have a measure of leaven and corruption in them. It's only God's virtue in us that can make us virtuous.

I was thirty-seven years old when I finally died. I had a great deal of apparent success on my résumé. I had founded and built a church. I had established a Christian school and a regional food bank. I had become a revivalist. But through it all and in spite of it all, God had to break me, exhaust me, bring me to my knees to teach me that the victorious Christian life can only be lived through faith in the promises of God and not by human effort. Only the strengthening power of the Holy Spirit can bring victory for Christ.

——⇒•⇐——

IMPORTANT TAKEAWAYS FROM THIS CHAPTER

KEY THOUGHT: A hard heart will always blame others for its own failures.

KEY WORD: Faith

KEY INSIGHT: God can break up the hard ground of unbelief and sow the seeds of faith. This happens when you take time to fast and pray for the lives of others. In the process you come into the life and power of God.

Chapter Three

PRAYING FOR STRENGTH

D O YOU FEEL as if you have only a little bit of strength? Are your weaknesses more pronounced than your strengths?

You are not alone. What may surprise you is that God does not require a huge amount of strength, nor does He shun our human weakness! We are His instruments—it is God who sculpts a masterpiece from our human fragility.

Hudson Taylor was a missionary and wonderful man of God. Prayer was the foundation of his life and his ministry. He once said, "God chose me because I was weak enough. God does not do his great works by large committees. He trains somebody to be quiet enough, and little enough, and then he uses him."[1]

Ray Buker, an Olympic runner, began his junior year at Bates in the fall of 1920. For the first time since the war the college entered a team into the New England cross-country event held in Boston at the Franklin Park course. Ray was a member of that team. It was a strange course, and although it had some gentle slopes, it had none of the steep hills that were characteristic of all his cross-country races in Maine. At about a mile from the finish Ray was so far behind the leaders that he was convinced that humanly speaking he could never place, even if he used his sprint for the last part of the race.

He prayed, telling the Lord that perhaps it was not His will that he should win and that he didn't know how he could. The Lord answered, "Start to sprint." Ray replied, "Lord, You know that one can't sprint for a mile!" He felt that God's answer entered his soul: "You obey Me, and you will see what I can do."

Ray began to sprint. He soon drew even with the leaders—and finished first.[2]

I believe that the church—the testimony of Christ in America today—has a little strength. We're not anywhere near as strong and powerful as we think we are.

In some ways our voices are largely marginalized. We have perhaps, and rightly so in our generation, been cast out as salt to be trodden under the feet of men. It would seem that the conviction of sin is no longer in the house of God.

The focus of much of the preaching in America in the last two decades turned away from the actual work of the cross of Jesus Christ and toward the gratification of self. Because of that the church has been left crippled and depleted in many ways.

How do we turn it around? I believe the beginning of a spiritual awakening is the humility to finally admit our condition and stop boasting about what we are not! Instead, as we turn to the Lord in prayer with willing hearts to follow Him, we will see that our "little strength" is no longer an albatross around our necks.

Can God use our weakened condition? Is a little bit of strength enough?

Revelation 3:7–13 says:

> And to the angel [or that means the messenger, the pastor] of the church in Philadelphia write, "These things says He who is holy, He who is true, 'He who has the key of David, He who opens and no one shuts, and shuts and no one opens': 'I know your works. See, I have set before you an open door, and no one can shut it; for you have a little strength, have kept My word, and have not denied My name. Indeed I will make those of the synagogue of Satan, who say they are Jews and are not, but lie—indeed I will make them come and worship before your feet, and to know that I have loved you. Because you have kept My command to persevere, I also will keep you from the hour of trial which shall come upon the whole world, to test those who dwell on the earth. Behold, I am coming quickly! Hold fast what you have, that no one may take your crown. He who overcomes, I will make him a pillar in the temple of My God, and he shall go out no more. I will write on him the name of My God and the name of the city of My God, the New Jerusalem, which comes down out of heaven from My God. And I will write on him My new name. He who has an ear, let him hear what the Spirit says to the churches.'"

I want you to take a close look at this verse—and He says, "I know your works. See, I have set before you an open door, and no one can shut it; for you have a little strength, have kept My word, and have not denied My name."

Jesus is telling us, "I have set before you an open door that no one can close." Did you hear that? The Lord is inviting you and me into a place where the impossible becomes possible. It's a place of victory—a place where God fights the battle, a battle that you could never win in your own strength.

When our "little strength" is coupled with prayer and faith, we can be assured that the Lord will lead us exactly where He wants us to be and we will do what He wants us to do.

The Lord is not asking us to come up with another committee. He's not asking us to craft some strategy to win our cities. He's not asking us to get together and picket and demonstrate for righteousness. No! Instead, the Lord is asking each one of us to rise up in the smallness of our strength because He has set before us an open door that no man can shut!

The little strength that you have can either make you cower in fear, or it can make you confident that God's strength and power working through you is all you need!

Many people try to refute Christianity. They use science, human reasoning, the exaltation of self, and other philosophies to try and dissuade people from believing in the gospel. But the one thing that no one can refute is the testimony of Christ lived out in the believer. God changes lives—and sometimes that change is dramatic.

The testimony of God over the children of Israel was powerful, not only to God's people but to the Egyptians and those who witnessed the miracles and the power of God on display. When the Lord brought His people out of Egypt, there was no question that the heavens and everything on the earth were subject to Him. God's faithfulness was on display and present in the midst of His people.

Sadly—even after all the miracles God's people had seen over the years—when the time came to cross the border and claim the place of promise that God had given them, they cowered in their own littleness! Instead of walking through the open door in God's strength, they ran in fear that their little strength was no match for the giants in the land.

The children of Israel forgot who God was, and instead of relying on Him to be their strength, they turned inward and were overcome with fear! Their unbelief said, "God's brought me this far, and He can bring me no further."

Whenever you turn inward, you are in trouble! You need to turn upward—you need to raise your hands to heaven and pray for strength to walk through the open doors that He has set before you. Though your strength is small, you are invited to arise and pass through into a place of victory that is already prepared for you.

We don't have to fight for it; the fight has already been won. We have to enter into it by faith.

NOT BY MIGHT, NOR BY POWER, BUT BY MY SPIRIT

When I talk about praying for strength to go through open doors, I'm talking about living a life that can only be explained by the supernatural presence of God. It's about moving beyond ourselves. We are not to muscle our way through our Christian life. Our inner strength will get us nowhere! The Christian life is lived through the power of Christ.

God's Word gives us three things to consider when God presents us with an open door into His presence and plan for our lives. The Book of Psalms says the blessings of God are given to those who have recognized their own weaknesses and have turned away from the world's influence and turned to God for help.

Three directives

1. "Walketh not in the counsel of the ungodly" (Ps. 1:1, KJV). In light of the father whose son was demon possessed, the moment he stepped away from the crowd (*ungodly*)—those whose lives were morally wrong, lawless, and unrighteous— the strongholds of wrong thinking could be broken in his life. The influence of the crowds, their arguments and their complaining, could no longer be a persuasive power over him. He had chosen to walk with Christ and away from the corrupt company that fed into his discontent. Christ was now able to begin speaking into his life about his own hard heart and the resident unbelief that filled it.

2. "Nor standeth in the way of sinners" (v. 1, KJV). The term *sinners* in the Hebrew writings has the same connotation as the word *sin* in the Greek, literally meaning to miss the mark, like an archer who shoots his arrows at the target but keeps missing the bull's-eye. In real terms it means a person who keeps missing a real relationship with God because of the wrong relationships the person is involved in.

   This father had been missing the mark for years (as seen by the answer he gave Jesus regarding how long his son had been possessed). But now he turned around 180 degrees (see my book *The 180-Degree Christian*), stepping away from the cantankerous crowd and choosing instead to walk with Christ.

3."Nor sitteth in the seat of the scornful" (v. 1, KJV). When a person sits around and scorns others, the result is a personal consequence of rejection in the person's own heart. In other words, after the crowds have gone home, the scorner is left carrying the full weight of ridicule and scorn in his or her own conscience. Once the father was away from the influence of the crowd, Jesus was able to reveal to him just how broken his relationship with God was.

The father's brazen accusations against the disciples and their failed attempts to deliver his son were actually accusations against God. Jesus knew that if this father would follow Him away from the crowd's influence, two things would happen: First, Jesus would be able to reveal to this father his bankrupted faith and spiritual weakness. Second, Christ would *open the door* of faith and God's blessings for him.

When Jesus said to the father, "If thou canst believe, all things are possible to him that believeth" (Mark 9:23, KJV), the *open door* was presented to him.

Jesus gave the father the opportunity to recognize his own weakness and depravity and to immediately lay hold of the offer of Christ to believe and step through the open door! "And straightway the father of the child cried out, and said with tears, Lord, I believe; help thou mine unbelief" (Mark 9:24, KJV). The father's response was exactly what Jesus was looking for. It was the confession of a man convicted in his heart of his own sin and inability, and by it God's open door of deliverance was presented, and the father walked through it.

God's glory can be found by praying and believing—it's not our intellect or skill—and only His power can achieve the miraculous. We've been robbed in this church age because we have moved away from the miraculous into the natural. In many churches and ministries today, marketing gurus, human intellect, and business acumen have seemed to replace God's power and direction. Why is this? Simply put, you don't need anything of God to preach what they preach. You don't need a living Word.

Much of what you hear preached in churches today is mental ascent. If you believe in this or that truth and put your hand to the plow, you will change. It's all in the natural. And not surprisingly there is no real transformation and no real open door of a supernatural God. God's open doors are always miraculous, and it requires prayer and faith to go through them.

There is a time when belief must be translated into action. If you believe, even simply, then you must get up and go through the doors God sets before you!

God's revelation to John went on to say, "I will make those who are of the synagogue of Satan, who claim to be Jews though they are not, but are liars—I will make them come and fall down at your feet and acknowledge that I have loved you" (Rev. 3:9, NIV).

I believe the Lord is saying, in so many words, "I will do something in your life so profound that game players, those who are not genuine with the things of God, will stand aghast at what I am able to do through you." In other words, when you walk through God's open doors, you will have a testimony, and that testimony of what God has done in your life is so powerful that it will make unbelievers want to know your God!

I hear the Lord saying, "I will do something through you so profound that it will expose their religious-ism as bankrupt." In Revelation 3:12–13 (NASB) the Lord goes on to say, "He who overcomes, I will make him a pillar in the temple of My God, and he will not go out from it anymore; and I will write on him the name of My God, and the name of the city of My God, the new Jerusalem, which comes down out of heaven from My God, and My new name. He who has an ear, let him hear what the Spirit says to the churches."

I believe the Spirit is still speaking to the churches, and He is speaking to you and me. *Overcoming* refers to overcoming the fear of going through the doors that God has set before us. By honoring those who courageously go through the doors, God supports the testimony of who He is through the people, the pillars of the temple, who support Him. There will be no more vacillating between victory and defeat. God says clearly that He is going to bring us in and make us solid in faith.

There will be no more "I believe; I don't believe. I believe; I don't believe." No more coming in and going out, coming in and going out. No more going to an altar on Sunday and claiming to believe and by Monday no longer believing. The concept is that God will do something in you that settles the question forever in your heart. You will be a man or woman of faith who believes steadfastly that God will do what He says He will do.

As pillars, we make declarations to others that what God has done for us He will do for others. Furthermore, it's a merciful message to those who only have a little strength, the people who believe God's Word and have not denied Him but have yet to go through the door He has set before them—into the strength that God offers.

The Open Door

What is God's open door? There are many! Essentially it is walking in the way that His Word would have us walk. The courage to forgive your enemies is an open door. Reconciling a broken relationship is another. Stepping out to talk to that unbelieving friend that the Lord has put on your mind is an open door. Speaking up for a victim or helping someone in need can be an open door. Confronting a family member in love regarding something the person is doing that is harming him or her is yet another door. An open door can be anything that the Lord is calling you to do, and you need strength to walk through it! Open doors are never easy to go through in our own strength and reasoning—that's why you need to be in prayer and you need to have faith to step through that door in the Lord's power.

It's been a very long journey to bring me to the point where if the Lord says to me, "Walk through this door," I simply do it. I don't question or balk anymore. He has proved too faithful on all other occasions for me to doubt Him now. At this season in my life I'm not afraid of something flopping. It's His strength that's going to make it happen—not mine. Likewise it's His glory that will be revealed in it—not mine.

And the Lord has told me to do a lot of things. One particular open door that the Lord wanted me to walk through was to "love your neighbor as yourself" (Matt. 22:39).

Why that? Of course we are commanded to love our neighbor—it comes right after loving God with all our heart. It's important. And it's not an easy thing to do. But for me, it was especially hard. In fact, earlier in my life, when the Lord told me to do this, I thought it defied reason—*my* reasoning, that is! I had a hard time loving people because I didn't love myself. In fact, I really was quite angry with people. When you loathe yourself, how can you love others? But God is ever faithful and ever patient. He showed me how to love my neighbor when I didn't even love myself. He said, "You must come to the point that you love the work I am doing in you. That's the self I want you to love."

The key to loving yourself and others is not in a human sense. The Lord taught me that it is about loving what He is doing in my life and others. It's about seeing myself, and others, in the light of Jesus Christ. Each person you meet was created by God—in His image! When we start looking at people this way, we have a new perspective. God loves that person you work with; God loves that person who has annoyed you; God loves that difficult family member. And just as the Lord is working in your life, He wants to work in their lives as well! Loving the Christ in me is easy to do. I love the work that He has done. That's why we can love our enemies and forgive those who have hurt us—because the Lord made and loves those people and wants them to know their Creator just as you know Him. When God revealed that to me, the puzzle was solved.

If we are in love with our own hearts apart from Christ in us, something is terribly wrong. As contrary as it is to the world's humanistic belief system, there is nothing redeemable in our natural hearts absent from God. There is nothing much worth loving. Christ in us—that's worth all our love. We should love the person Christ is making us. And we need to understand that our neighbors, both the unsaved and saved, are loved by God and that He wants to work in their lives as well!

I can surely say that if you loathe yourself, it is not possible to share the love of God! What I did before God shared this with me was develop a view of others that reflected how I saw myself. When we look at someone and think, "You are a loathsome, despicable person in desperate need of redemption," how does the love of God dwell in us? And how on earth can we share our testimony? See how easy it is to fall into this sinful thought pattern—especially for Christians? We all need God's redemption. We all are created in His image. And God wants a relationship with all of us.

———————

I remember clearly that I once said aloud in the super-market, "I hate people!"

People were what caused me to feel insecure and run out of classrooms when they turned their attention to me. I believed that people put unrealistic demands on me. That's why I used to retreat to my mom and dad's cottage on a lake in the Canadian wilderness and be completely alone and completely at peace. I didn't need or want anyone around. The way I saw it, people were the problem. People were a source of pain to me. That's why it is so amazing that God turned me around 180 degrees. Now people are a great joy to me, and the only pain I feel when it comes to people is that they might not get to heaven. If they don't make it, that will pain me.

I have seen the witness of Christ in many ways over my lifetime. I've seen miracles, particularly overseas. I've seen tens of thousands come to Christ in one moment. I've seen genocide stopped. I've seen great sweeps of God's almighty hand.

"But what's the greatest miracle of them all?" you ask.

"That I love people," I would be compelled to answer.

To me the whole journey has been made worthwhile by this one truth. And it's not a feigned thing. I never learned how to fake love in a convincing way. I pray with six or seven guys from the church every morning, and each time we close off, I say, "I love you." And I mean it.

Years ago, decades, actually, I had a disagreement that ended a friendship with a Christian man in Canada. We were in ministry together during the first five or six years of my salvation and had been close. We witnessed together and played our guitars and sang Christian songs in coffeehouses. Three or four months before I began writing this book, I re-established contact with him. We talked over the telephone for quite a while, catching up. When we were wrapping up, I said to him, "I love you." I didn't give it any thought. It just came out: "I love you."

There was a long silence on the line. Then, when he tried to speak, all he could do was stammer. "Ah, ah..." He struggled for words. He was that taken aback. Finally he said, "I love you too, Carter."

I had forgotten how improbable it would seem to people who had known me before for those words to come out of my mouth now or ever.

The man he remembered was very different from the man he was talking to on the telephone all these years later. The man he remembered could never say, "I love you." I didn't realize until this recent conversation that he didn't know how to say it either. Neither one of us expected to hear the other say such a thing back in the day, and we probably didn't expect to ever hear it.

The fact that I can genuinely express love now is an open door that I walked through and for which I am eternally grateful.

———❖———

Of the many, many open doors that God has for you, the most prominent is the leading of God for your life, His plan being lived out in your life and bringing Him glory. The willingness to forgive is an important door to go through. Through forgiveness God is glorified. The willingness to believe that you can be a good husband and father, or a good wife and mother, is something that brings God glory. In all the open doors that God gives us, He says, "Follow Me through this."

Again and again, God has called me to go to places I was not qualified to go to and do things I was not qualified to do. I don't have certificates on the wall in my office because I might be tempted to believe that I accomplished something on my own. I was offered an honorary doctorate a few years ago, and I refused it for just that reason.

The open doors God sets before us require prayer and faith. We already know from Hebrews 11:6 that we can't please Him without faith. Hebrews also describes how Abraham had an open door placed before him by God. He had no children, as Sarah was barren. They were much too old in the natural sense to even have kids. Yet God called them to parent the nation Israel. God set an open door before Noah to save his family, and he built an ark on faith. As ridiculous as that looked to observers—after all, they had never even seen rain—Noah's entire household was saved. And even so he struggled with drinking. One miracle doesn't solve all things. Even in Noah's imperfection, when God set before him an open door, he obeyed.

Surrendering our lives to Christ is stepping through an open door in faith. I led my mother and father to Christ. As a pastor, I never try to lay a guilt trip on people, but I can say, "Here's the door. Come through it. Unless, and until, you pass through that door, you won't know the power of God in your life."

The Lord came to Gideon and called him a mighty man of resource and valor. Gideon, who by his own description was the least of the least, walked through the door that God opened for him to save his people from the Midianites.

Are you willing to walk through the open door that God has set before you?

———❖———

I became a door greeter and worship leader at the church Teresa and I attended. Eventually I felt the Lord's calling to start a Bible study in a little country church. I didn't know anything about teaching the Word of God, but I started the study anyway.

Needing a place to hold the study, I found a church building and went to the board members of the non-Bible-believing church and appealed to them. I told them exactly who I was and what I wanted to do. This was a church that met for one hour on Sundays and had no other activities during the week. I asked to rent the church, but they decided to give me free use as long as we took care of their property and left it in as good a shape as or better shape than how we found it.

I printed thousands of fliers and mailed them to everybody in the area. Shortly thereafter a fellow from Ottawa called me. He was from the Gideons and told me that they had just replaced the English-language Bibles in a big hotel with new French-English bilingual versions, and he had a garage full of the old Bibles. "Do you want any of them?" he asked.

"I'll take them all," I told him. So I began giving away a Bible to everyone who came to the Bible study. Each week, I had everyone open to the Gospel of John, the book that first introduced me to Christ. I taught line by line. Where I left off each week, I started the next week. No training. No seminary. No instruction in how to lead a small group. Just God's calling.

People started to get saved, and the study began to grow. Before long they said, "We're a church, and you're our pastor." I was OK with everything except the pastor part. So I set out to find a pastor who would come and minister to these people. I went to several organizations and finally settled on one particular Pentecostal group. I spoke to the district head of the denomination, and he asked me if I wanted to be the pastor.

"No," I replied. "I have a good career as a cop. And I'm just not interested."

"Would you be willing to hold the church for six months until we find a pastor?" he asked.

"I could do that, I suppose."

So I pastored this group of people, and the study continued to grow in number, so much so that we moved into a larger facility. God spoke to me often, saying, "I've set before you an open door." But my career with the Ottawa police was secure. I had a great job, and I was advancing rapidly. I was well paid, and I was happy with my choice of career.

Interestingly enough, our new facility was a small hotel in town. It was owned by a very colorful lady. She was the closest thing to Rahab the harlot I had ever encountered. Our "church" met in the bar since it wasn't open for business on Sunday morning and it could seat a lot of people. We turned the bandstand into our worship and preaching platform! The hotel owner would attend our services dressed in a red floor-length negligee and floor-length satin robe. She loved what we were doing, although we could never quite get her to the altar. As if that scene were not bizarre enough, the local Catholic priest, displeased with our little church's growing popularity, sent his parishioners out of mass one Sunday morning to get in their cars, surround the hotel during our service, and blow their horns. This went on for over fifteen minutes.

God began telling me to take charge of this small group of people, quit my job, and live on $340 per week. All I could think of was that $340 per week wouldn't cover my bills. It was ludicrous to consider. It was financial suicide to look at it in the natural. The thought of pastoring this church was the opposite of what any sane person would do. My career was taking off like a rocket, and I was receiving more respect *from my fellow police officers all the time. Giving all that up would mean losing the money, the security, my government pension, and their respect.*

But it was an open door God had set before me. I was preaching in the hotel bar one cold winter Sunday morning about giving our all to God. I believed that with all my heart. As I was speaking, I glanced out the window and saw three or four little brown sparrows pecking away at the snow. I couldn't see any seeds or anything else that might be attracting them, but they kept pecking anyway.

Then God spoke to me again. "Aren't you worth more than they?" He asked. "I care for them and provide for them. Do you not believe—do you not believe—that I will care all the more for you? I've set before you an open door. Do you not trust Me enough to go through it?"

It was on that day that my heart started turning toward God's call to go through that open door.

Nothing can bring about the tears of brokenness more than the revelation of your own weaknesses. The father's snarky attitude with Jesus' disciples had now melted into a pool of spiritual weakness and ineptness. With tears streaming down his face, he cried out from his heart—he was no longer concerned about the thoughts or views of others; this was now a confrontation between God and a broken man.

The father answered Jesus, "I believe; help my unbelief!"

When the father said, "I believe," he was literally saying that he was convinced no earthly man could set his son free—it had to be God and His divine power. This was the beginning of his faith; the door was open, and he could walk through it.

After telling Jesus he believed, the father went on to ask the Lord to help him in his unbelief! The man knew that his help could only come from God. But he had a distrust of being helped by humanity. After all, no one person had been able to help him or his son. The father was convicted in his heart that only God could set his son free, but his lack of confidence in Jesus was because He was a man.

With one foot through the *open door*, he needed help in taking the next vital step of trusting God through His sent Messiah, Jesus Christ. It was an internal battle—a battle that was even tougher than his son being bound by Satan.

The father made an honest confession from a broken heart, and it carried him across the finish line of faith!

My dear fellow Christian, God looks upon the heart. He looks upon your heart. Jesus saw the father's battle and dispelled his unbelief by performing a miracle of deliverance for his possessed son. It is here in the heart where man believes (Rom. 10:10) and where faith in God is rewarded. This father's prayer came from a place of little strength in himself, yet it was enough with God to propel him through an open door of impossibility to the reality and freedom of God's power.

WHAT DOOR DO YOU NEED TO GO THROUGH?

What door are you facing right now? What has God called you to do that you have been afraid to do? Are you looking at your littleness or relying on the Lord's strength to walk you through that open door? It's God's supernatural strength that will get the job done. Any job that will please Him is worth doing.

I've already mentioned several times that the open doors God puts before us often lead to places where we are not qualified or credentialed to go. The open doors God sets before us oftentimes lead to places where we don't *want* to go! Maybe that's what you are facing right now. The Lord has shown you a door that He has opened and that He wants you to walk through—yet you really don't want to. Listen, my friend, I've been there, and I can honestly tell you that as you step out in prayer and in faith, the Lord will bring you to the other side, and it will become a blessing to you. In fact, it's often the doors that we don't want to step through that the Lord uses to bring about the greatest good in our lives!

I'm sure you know this already, but the Lord doesn't set out the whole plan for us at one time. He has us step out in faith and only gives us what is needed to take the next step. That's how the Lord works. It really comes down to prayer and faith. Prayer is vital—you need to be in constant communication with the Lord to know where He is leading you and what He is saying to you! You need to be in His Word as well. Finally you need to trust God. As much as we think we know what is best for our lives, the truth is that we don't! Left to our natural selves, we have no clue what is best for ourselves, let alone anyone else. However, God knows you intimately. He made you. He knows how you are wired. In fact, God knows you better than you know yourself. He loves you, and He died for you. His plan for your life is good. The Lord is worthy of your trust!

Will you trust Him as you walk through your open door?

——◆◆——

That wasn't the last I heard of my decision. People thought I was crazy. My father said to me, "When there is no food to feed your family and there is no milk in the fridge for your kids, don't come to me. I will not help you. What you are doing is foolish." That was a bitter pill to swallow.

I had Christian men say to me, "You're leading your family into a place of jeopardy." Yet I knew it was an open door. More importantly I knew that it was God's open door. I said to my critics, "In the natural it makes no sense. All I can tell you is that I hear God calling me to walk through this door, and I've decided to go."

There were two Christian police officers on the Ottawa Police Department who supported me in my conversion and helped steady me as I took my first baby believer steps. When I made the decision to leave the police department and enter full-time ministry, however, they both opposed what I was doing—and were quite vocal about it. They questioned my Christian responsibilities to my wife and three children, as other believers had. "You're going to bring your family into hardship," they complained. Then, when they realized I wasn't going to be turned back from it, the older of the two came to me alone and shared, "I once felt God calling me to become a pastor, and I didn't go."

It was his way of saying, "Good luck; Godspeed," without literally coming out and endorsing what I was doing. When he spoke those words, it suddenly became clear to me why he had argued so vehemently against my choice. My going through the door God had set before me made him feel condemned for not going through the door God had set before him. He had argued that I could have been a good witness as a Christian cop and done many good things. However, that's the path he had chosen for his life, and indeed, his Christian walk blessed many, many people. I never would have condemned him for that. He was a nurturing kind of guy, full of compassion. He would have made a great pastor. But he wouldn't go through the open door that the Lord had set before him. And he only admitted it after I refused to turn back.

When I had about a week to go before my last day at the Ottawa Police Department, the word of my leaving was out, and lots of people were perplexed because I had attained a high-profile position, especially for a man of my age. I came out of the elevator one day and came face to face with an officer in uniform. I knew who he was, but I can't say I knew him well. There were nearly seven hundred people working at the Ottawa Police Department at the time. But I knew him well enough to know he was not a believer.

He reached out and hugged me. No one hugs in the French-Canadian Ontario-Quebec National Capital Region in public! He stepped back and looked at me through misty eyes and said, "I don't agree with what you believe.

"But you've got guts, man. I respect that."

As he got on the elevator and went his way, I stood there for a moment, realizing the first encouragement I had received to step out in faith came from a nonbeliever.

I was aware that there appeared to be a cliff on the other side of my open door. I wasn't blind. I knew that God would need to sustain me. I felt like Peter stepping out of the boat. There was nothing in the natural to support me. I knew that if God did not support me, I was finished. But from the moment I stepped out of the boat, the journey God put before me was amazing to behold.

———

There will always be a gaggle of prophets who will come out and predict loss if you go through the door. I've described already the way many of those voices came out and tried to chase me away from the open doors God set before me in Canada. I could cite a thousand more instances of voices up to this present day predicting loss and doom when I move toward an open door God has set before me. Some of those voices even come from inside my own church.

First Corinthians 16:9 says, "A great door for effective work has opened to me, and there are many who oppose me" (NIV).

Opposition to the work of Christ comes from two directions: Satan and people. If the devil can marginalize you into becoming merely a spectator in the work of Christ, then he has already won half the battle. And on the other side of the coin, if it's not the devil bringing opposition against you, then he will use people to oppose you (Phil. 3:18).

The crowd surrounding the father with the possessed son was spectators observing and criticizing from a distance the disciples' efforts to cast out the demon. Spectator opposition is a huge peer pressure that hinders others from participating in the work of God.

After the Israelites had crossed the Red Sea and were at the border of the Promised Land, Moses sent in twelve spies to gather information concerning the place they were about to inherit. Ten of the twelve Israelite spies returned with negative reports, and the force of this negativity spread like wildfire throughout the camp. Their report was in opposition to the promises of God, which resulted in gross unbelief, paralyzing the entire people. Only two, Joshua and Caleb, believed God and were willing to be participants with Him and not remain spectators. They believed God could take them into the Promised Land and conquer all of their enemies immediately.

Israel failed that day to go through the *open door* because of the resistance and *opposition* of the people because of unbelief.

Don't let opposition deter you from walking by faith. Many people, including believers, live by their own wits instead of by faith. But when you don't live by faith, God cannot lead you. So we make choices: "I'm living in the strength of my family." "I'm living in the halls of academia." "I'm living in the success of my career."

The decision to give one's life over to Christ is a supernatural decision. If it's an intellectual decision, it will not lead to a transformed life. If I can't be "all in," I don't want to be in at all. If my choice is to live in the natural realm, I wouldn't stay in the ministry. I'd go get a job doing something else. I can't imagine dedicating my life to the service of the Lord and not crossing over into the supernatural. I know that many men and women do. Many Christians pride themselves on living, worshipping, teaching, and doing good works in the natural. Their water isn't living, though; it's lifeless.

Walk by faith—go through that open door that the Lord is calling you to—and you will not regret it!

Praying for Strength to Walk Through Your Open Door

Do you need strength to walk through God's open door for your life? Here are some powerful prayer approaches to take when opposition arises!

First, in prayer, rely on God for your *future*. This will increase your faith in God and circumvent the words and attitudes of opposition that come your way.

Second, in prayer, accept God's word by *faith*, and walk in His direction with confidence and courage. There is nothing like the Word of God to overcome all doubt and opposition.

Third, in prayer, do not be intimidated with *fear* when inundated with difficulties. He will bring you through every opposition by His wisdom and power.

Finally, in prayer, allow the Holy Spirit's voice to be heard over the voice of *failure*. In God's economy setbacks are springboards and stepping-stones to take you to the other side of the storm. The devil uses failure to condemn, but when you hear God speaking to your heart, you will overcome the devil's opposition.

This book is an open door for anyone who reads it. It's an invitation to the supernatural life that only God can provide. I call it becoming addicted to glorifying God. We just need to pray and believe. I know for certain that nothing happens through unbelief. It's like the old sports maxim "You miss 100 percent of the shots you don't take." If given the choice, I would rather step out in faith and fail than not step out at all.

So many people are afraid to look stupid. They really don't believe that God is going to support them. As a result, they don't take the step. They don't go through the doors that God sets before them. In our church I can see a growing movement and willingness to step out into the supernatural power of God. It's always been God's pattern to show Himself in what He does through His people. He's not calling us to follow a God we cannot fully embrace as infinite, omnipotent, omniscient, and omnipresent.

Without that we become an entity with an argument. That's largely what the church in the world has come to be. Every church on every corner has a viewpoint on certain theological perspectives, but there really is no power there. The power is in the blood. Our churches today seem helpless to stem the tide of divorce and failed marriages. We should declare the modern statistics about marriage intolerable.

When 120 people spilled out of the Upper Room and brought 3,000 people into the kingdom in a single day, it was only because they were supernaturally empowered. Today so much of the church has settled for good arguments, but good arguments don't capture souls.

There is nothing mysterious about the supernatural; it simply allows people to do things they would not be able to do in their own strength.

Keep it simple. Pray, believe, and obey. How much theology do you need to give half your sandwich to a hungry man? How much Hebrew do you need to be able to read the Word of God? Yet to bestow grace and mercy to a brother or sister in need is to obey the supernatural order of God.

The church was born in the supernatural. The supernatural is the only place it can live, much less grow. Revival in the years ahead will be directly proportional to the degree Christians prayerfully seek the strength to go through the open doors the

Lord sets before them, strength that only comes through His indwelling spirit.

All of us need to be comfortable in the presence of Christ and uncomfortable in our sin. That's the Holy Spirit at work. The religious person of Christ's day and the contemporary Christian in name only will be uncomfortable with the indwelling Spirit of Christ and the things Jesus asks us to do. I am willing to believe that what God did for sinners in biblical times He will do for you and me right now. God is merciful.

If you scream at God the way I screamed at God, I believe He will gently whisper back, "I love you," just as He whispered to me. I believe if you walk through the doors that God sets before you, He will be faithful to walk beside you, guide you, and never forsake you—just as He has done for me. As unequipped and unprepared as we might be to walk through a door God sets before us, as sinful as we might be at any moment of our lives, He loves us through it all. All we need to do is *pray and simply believe.*

——◆——

One day early in our ministry years Teresa and I drove to a park and stopped the car so we could chat by ourselves. "Please tell me everything I have done to hurt you," I begged her. "I will listen to the best of my ability. I won't argue or defend. I want to hear you, really hear everything that's on your heart." This was the first time since becoming a Christian that I totally dropped my defenses, dropped my guard, and was willing to absorb whatever Teresa had to unload on me.

It was like walking through an open door and laying down the sword and shield I always carried with me to deflect criticism. I was anxious to leave all of that stuff behind, but Teresa hadn't found resolution yet. My impatience to let bygones be bygones didn't help heal the damage I had inflicted. Thank God she trusted me to go through the open door I set before her. Not only did she go through it; she charged through it.

She let everything out—her entire list of grievances. It was exactly what I needed to hear. Thanks be to God that He kept me silent. For the first time, I took the shots and didn't shoot back. I didn't defend myself. To argue back against the things she was accusing me of would have been to defend the un-Christlike behaviors of a man Christ was working to re-create in His image. It would have been like trying to hold on to the bad stuff for whatever good could have come from it—which was none.

God rested His gentle hand on my fear muscle and allowed me to hear what Teresa needed to say. I had never listened that way before, and I've never stopped listening that way since. If someone approaches me now and says, "I don't like your preaching," I genuinely want to know why and explore together what the Lord might be doing in that moment. I might even bring others into the conversation and find if there is validity in the complaint. In my days as a young preacher, a hockey game might have broken out on the spot.

Teresa got it all out that day. I listened, never once picking up my self-made sword and shield. When she finished, I'm sure she was ready to hear my defense. Instead, I took a deep breath and said, "There's more."

"No," she said. "I think I covered it all."

"I am guilty of even more than what you said," I confessed. "But there is nothing for me to say except to ask your forgiveness. I can't make it right. I can't make it go away. I can't change the past."

In those early years, anytime we exchanged accusations, I had a comeback, even when she had me dead to rights. "Yeah," I would say, "maybe I did. But you did…," and out would come one of my tired old grievances. This time, that day in the park, God actually told me to take what she was saying and to not throw anything back.

"Take your responsibility," he said. "You are the covering on this home and your family. If the enemy breaches the walls, it's your fault, not hers."

Going through that door of vulnerability requires trusting God to put the fractured pieces back together in a way that glorifies Him. Starting through the door and laying down my self-made weapons looked like weakness to me. But on the other side of that door, God turned it to strength. Teresa tells the story that at the moment I asked for her forgiveness, the Holy Spirit came on her and said, "What right do you have to carry a sword in your hand?" She describes how she obeyed, and in the car at that moment, she put her sword back in its sheath and never drew it out again.

Collectively, in our weakness, and through much prayer and faith, we walked through the open door that the Lord had for our relationship and walked right into His victory.

————⟫•⟪————

Important Takeaways From This Chapter

KEY THOUGHT: God has set an open door before you!

KEY WORD: Strength

KEY INSIGHT: There will always be opposition from the devil and from people to keep you from moving forward in the things of God. Remember, God uses setbacks and turns them into springboards, giving you strength to go through the open door for your life.

Chapter Four

PRAYING FOR SERVING

P ATRICK HENRY SHOUTED, "Give me liberty, or give me death."
The next generation shouted, "Give me liberty."
The present generation shouts, "Give me."[1]

━━◆◈◆━━

We are all born, without exception, selfish in the core of our beings. This self-focus is entrenched in our sinful nature, and though there are compassionate people in society, the general human tendency is not to be focused on the well-being of other people.

Compassion *is* the focus of God. "For God so loved the world that he gave his one and only Son, that whoever believes in him shall not perish but have eternal life" (John 3:16, NIV). In the same way, as God's children, we are to be more concerned about other people than ourselves. We are to love and serve others—God's entire ministry to us is about others. And when I say, "Love and serve others," that doesn't mean just our friends! Jesus was clear when He said, "You have heard that it was said, 'Love your neighbor and hate your enemy.' But I tell you, love your enemies and pray for those who persecute you, that you may be children of your Father in heaven. He causes his sun to rise on the evil and the good, and sends rain on the righteous and the unrighteous. If you love those who love you, what reward will you get? Are not even the tax collectors doing that? And if you greet only your own people, what are you doing more than others? Do not even pagans do that? Be perfect, therefore, as your heavenly Father is perfect" (Matt. 5:43–48, NIV).

I have always believed that it is impossible to claim, "I am in Christ, and Christ is in me," and not be lovingly and compassionately invested in the physical, spiritual, and emotional health and well-being of other people—no matter who they are.

In 1997, about three years after coming to Times Square Church, I was invited to speak at Sullivan prison in Fallsburg, New York. I was ushered into a section of the prison with about sixty "lifers." These sixty men, whose greatest ambition was to kill a cop— in this case, an ex-cop—had nothing left to lose. What would another life sentence matter to them? They were already going to die behind bars.

David Berkowitz led the worship that night. You might remember him as the infamous Son of Sam and the string of six murders he committed between July 29, 1976, and July 31, 1977, in New York City. David is serving six life sentences and has asked to never be paroled because of the responsibility he now feels for the murders he committed and injuries he caused. He is now a wonderful Christian man, totally in love with his Lord. He has a ministry to prisoners who come in so beaten up that they can't brush their own teeth. He brushes their teeth for them and helps them wash themselves as he tells them how much God loves them. I know the Holy Spirit was and is with David, yet further evidence that the Lord can save and completely transform anybody and anything.

With the auditorium doors locked behind us, I was there with two unarmed guards, one trumpet player from Times Square Church named Angelo, and the sixty aforementioned lifers. As soon as I got up to speak, I told them that I was an ex-cop. Angelo, who was seated behind me, muttered, "Uh-oh." Angelo, who was a former inmate himself, scolded me later about how dangerous it was for me to confess that I used to be a cop, especially to lifers. No sooner had I mentioned that I was a former cop than one of the prisoners from the back of the auditorium stood up, walked down the aisle, sat down directly in front of me, folded his arms, and glared at me.

"I'm not here because I've got nothing better to do," I told them. "I'm not here because I'm a do-gooder. I'm here because God loves you. I'm here because you can be free, even if you never leave these walls. Your prison is not built by men; your prison is a matter of the heart, and you are captive because you don't know the love God has for you. You don't know the freedom Christ died to give you."

When I finished speaking, I made an invitation. About eight men came forward. I hugged each one of them, one by one. It was a beautiful sight to see—a cop hugging men with life sentences. Every one of them was weeping and shaking like a baby. What a privilege it was to tell them that God loved them.

In Luke 4:18–19 Jesus quoted the words of Isaiah 61:1, saying, "The Spirit of the Lord is on me, because He has anointed me to proclaim good news to the poor. He has sent me to proclaim freedom for the prisoners and recovery of sight for the blind, to set the oppressed free, to proclaim the year of the Lord's favor" (NIV).

Jesus stood in the synagogue, opened the Scripture, and essentially said, "The Spirit of God is upon Me for you, and you, and you, and you…" There was no other reason the Spirit was upon Him except to alleviate human suffering and for the redemption of fallen humanity. Jesus' desire was to bring a fallen people into the knowledge of God and, ultimately, back to living with God for all eternity.

I've always believed it is impossible to say that "Christ is mine, and I am Christ's" yet remain self-absorbed. The apostle Paul, writing in 2 Timothy, warned that perilous times will come. "Men will be lovers of self," he wrote (2 Tim. 3:2, NASB). That self-love would be the underpinning of everything else he was about to write. Loving ourselves and giving ourselves preeminence in life automatically means that our relationships with others are a form of religion that lacks the power of God. Paul ultimately says turn away from self-serving religion. Any faith based on the life of Jesus Christ within us must be lived for the benefit and the sake of other people.

We can know in large measure the heart of God for people. I remember the story in Mark 8 where Jesus led the blind man away from the village of Bethsaida in order to restore his sight, which I think represents leading people away from a culture that confines and even tries to hijack the love of God and give credit to humankind for the things that God does. It's all about me, myself, and I, with no room left for God.

"When he had spit on the man's eyes and put his hands on him, Jesus asked, 'Do you see anything?' [The man] looked up and said, 'I see people; they look like trees walking around.' Once more Jesus put his hands on the man's eyes. Then his eyes were opened, his sight was restored, and he saw everything clearly. Jesus sent him home, saying, 'Don't even go into the village'" (Mark 8:23–26, NIV).

The man's sight was only partially restored at first. It wasn't until God touched him the second time that he saw clearly. That's how it often works in our walks with God. He continues to touch our eyes and our hearts as often as needed until we see clearly and love willingly, sincerely, and genuinely. If we allow Jesus to lead us down the path into a life of living for others, it will be a difficult journey.

———————

You might give up everything to the service of others in your life without any apparent recompense. Yet it is all part of learning to be given for others. Teresa and I were on Prince Edward Island once when I was preaching. We came home to find out our Canadian farmhouse had burned down. Everything we owned was gone. I remember the pain in my heart when the church that we had founded and given everything for seemed to close its hands of compassion.

It was a very hurtful moment in my life when people I had given so much for and cared for turned away when I needed them most. The Lord provided and met every one of our needs. Make no mistake about that. But God said to me clearly, "Carter, I've taught you in these classrooms of life that to be given for other people means giving up any expectation of personal reward or privilege. You are simply being given for them because you love them, not for what they can give you—even in times of great need."

Living for others brings us to places where we will be gravely wounded by people we are invested and believe in—as Joseph was, as David was. Living for others brings us to a place of forgiving those who have offended us, feeding those who have not provided for us, being kind to those whose words to us are unkind. You must believe me when I tell you that I have lived through all of this, more than once. It has been difficult and has stretched my strength to my limits. It has been so bad at times that I called out to God to provide strength to carry me. And He did carry me.

I've had to learn to pray for being a servant to others as much as I had to learn to pray for salvation, for new life, or for strength to preach. Then, as I was being led into ministry, I had to learn what ministry was all about. It has been truly amazing to see and experience firsthand what Jesus meant when He said that we must deny ourselves, take up our crosses, and *follow Him. Like so many others, I thought I knew. I picked up my own piece of wood and hopscotched down the road thinking how grand it was all going to be.*

—◆—

Living for others is a difficult journey, mostly because the devil will do everything in his power to stop it by convincing you that the world—and God, for that matter—revolves around *you.*

To be sure, not all people you serve will respond in love. In fact, you can pretty much expect betrayal to enter your life at some point, just as it entered Joseph's life. Don't be surprised if people close to you abandon you and pretend you don't exist. Or, when they do acknowledge your compassion, they might ascribe false and unflattering motives to your good works.

Yes, living for others is a difficult thing, but it is the way of the gospel. It's the way of the cross. It is the path to God's power.

Have you ever found yourself being accosted by overzealous sales reps? I have. I've been in places where I've literally had a group surrounding me, wanting me to buy their item. It can be exhausting. Jesus' disciples were surrounded, not by sales reps, but critical scribes questioning them nonstop. In Mark 9, when Jesus came down the mount, He asked the scribes, "What question ye with them?" (v. 16, KJV). I'm sure Jesus could see His disciples feeling harassed by all their questions. The father of the demon-possessed child, who was among the multitude, was perhaps disappointed in the lack of power displayed by Christ's disciples.

It is a fact; "unmet expectations" remains the leading reason why people become disappointed with God, church, marriage, business, and life in general. A wife may become disappointed in her husband simply because he did not match up to her perceived expectations she had before the marriage, or vice versa. Children disappoint parents, and parents disappoint children. It happens all the time. Living for others when overwhelming disappointments have shattered your world is difficult at best.

Jesus did three things to remove disappointment and restore faith in God. He knew this man needed empathy before He could demonstrate true sympathy. To sympathize would only yield to this man's disappointment and agree with it. Jesus would demonstrate true sympathy for the child only once the father addressed his own disappointments.

- First, He had the man go back and "remember" the point of disappointment in his life (v. 21).

- Second, living for others is allowing them to "talk about the offense" without you becoming defensive. Ultimately this man's disappointment was with God and therefore with Christ Himself. Jesus did not defend His Father's honor, nor did He defend the powerlessness of His disciples. Jesus was more interested in this man's healing than proving who was right or wrong. It was the most important issue other than setting the child free from demonic possession.

- Third, Jesus allowed this distraught father to identify his own need of God: "And straightway the father of the child cried out, and said with tears, Lord, I believe; help thou mine unbelief" (v. 24, kjv).

The beauty of the kingdom of God is that the diploma we receive for learning our lessons about living in service to others doesn't seem to match the courses required for graduation. How does betrayal by his family in Joseph's life, being sold off into slavery, being falsely accused of rape in an Egyptian leader's house, being falsely imprisoned, and being forgotten by people whom he helped while he was in prison produce Joseph's loving heart? How did all of that lead Joseph to a place where he was willing to forgive his brothers when they appeared before him?

How did all of that lead Joseph to open the storehouse of God to feed his betrayers and tell them not to be afraid? How did thirteen years of indescribable pain in Joseph's life lead him to be merciful to those who caused the pain? It is only the unnatural School of Christ that can teach us how to be given for the benefit of others in the midst of suffering by others' hands.

This really shouldn't surprise us. We don't learn to love people by being surrounded by people who love us. We don't learn patience by being given what we want when we want it. We don't learn to trust God when everything is going smoothly in our lives. It is through the difficult times in our lives that we build godly character and become more like Christ.

I'm not telling you all of this to scare you away from serving others. The truth is that when you live to serve others, it leads you into places where you are stretched beyond your natural ability to do what needs to be done according to the Word of God. And because of this, it leads you to a place where there needs to be a life other than your own that carries you through and gives you strength to be an ambassador for the mercy of God, forgiving those whom, in your flesh, you would be inclined to hate and never forgive.

Perhaps you, like me, had no idea that the cross of Christ would mean that people who promised to love you would deny you when you needed them most. People would lie about you and swear under oath that they never knew you. People who once said, "I love you," will tell you they don't even like you. People whom your hands reached out to in kindness are not going to be there in your time of need. You're going to be lied about, slandered, and vilified.

If God plans to use your life in any significant way, you'll need to endure the hazing of those you are serving! And you will be called to love them. This is precisely what Jesus promised Paul as He invited His newly converted persecutor to walk in the Word and serve his Creator. In Acts 9:16 Jesus promises that Paul will suffer much for following Him.

You'll be called to dip bread in the wine of your sacrifice and hand it across the table to your Judas. Believe me, if you follow Christ, truly follow Him, you will have at least one Judas in your life. It's not going to be easy. But if you and I are not willing to pass through this classroom that God has called us to, and pray to love and serve others, it will be impossible for us to grow in our faith.

Is it any wonder that, when such a profound state of self-lessness is required to truly follow God, so few choose that path? I was preaching on evangelism not very long ago when a woman approached the altar to give her life to Jesus Christ. With tears streaming down her face, she took off her wig and laid it on the platform. She was a man dressed as a woman, who had answered the call of Christ. These kinds of things would be impossible to believe were it not for the lessons God teaches in the classrooms of loving and giving ourselves up for others.

God will be God, even to the most ungodly among us. Better

said, God will be in His greatest glory in the midst of the most ungodly among us. Jonah couldn't bring himself to pray that God would be merciful to those who were professed enemies to the people of God. Yet to those who treated the people of God with contempt and cruelty, God was nonetheless merciful, especially merciful. It annoyed Jonah to no end. After God extended indescribable mercy to the people of Nineveh, Jonah sat on a hillside above the city, angry and grieved in his heart that God had not destroyed the people who had caused such pain to his own nation.

It is hard for some to admit, but how low has religiousness sunk when our hearts are saddened when our enemies turn to God? We'd rather call down fire upon them and see them burn in hell for all eternity than see them receive God's mercy—the same mercy, by the way, that He extended to us! We'd rather pound the pulpit with our fists and claim that their degrading and disgusting sin is abhorrent and intolerant to God than open our fists and lift open hands, crying hot tears and pleading with God to show them mercy and change them from the inside out.

We can too quickly become ambassadors of the other kingdom, Satan's kingdom of degenerate men's hearts masquerading as the religion of God. That's what Paul warned us about: a religion without power—something that displays an outward righteousness but is bankrupt when it comes to possessing the heart of God. I have walked the full course of this journey in my life, and there will be more classrooms I'll need to occupy. But I am confident, as Paul wrote, that God is able to keep those things I put into His hands until the day that I come home to Him.

The cross is all about others. "For God so loved the world, that he gave his only begotten Son..." (John 3:16, KJV). We need to embrace God's mercy to extend mercy. If we open our hearts, we will become an expression to others of Christ, who went to the cross with open arms and an open heart to receive all who would come to Him. By God's grace and lots of prayer, that is how our lives are going to finish—all about others.

I know why you got saved. That's important. But the question now becomes, Why are you living for Christ? What is your motivation for being part of the kingdom of God? Are you living for yourself, or are you willing to live for others? We must focus on others if we are to truly pray for others as Christ taught us to pray.

Without that focus on others, we will pray without ceasing for ourselves exclusively. "Give *me* my daily bread....Forgive *me*....Lead *me*....Deliver *me*....Protect *me*...." When we finally become secure and mature in Christ, we will go into the closet and pray for others to receive the bread they need, the freedom they need, the protection they need.

When our focus shifts from ourselves to others, everything changes.

LOVE OTHERS AS GOD LOVES YOU

God's Word is very clear about being "others-centered." Scripture tells us, "Greater love hath no man than this, that a man lay down his life for his friends" (John 15:13, KJV). This implies a complete giving of ourselves for other people, irrespective of whether there is any reciprocation. The Lord told us that if we do these things, His joy will be in us, and our joy will be full! Knowing we would need this driven home, Jesus said, "A new command I give you: Love one another. As I have loved you, so you must love one another" (John 13:34, NIV).

———

I am reminded again of the time decades ago when I was lying in bed crying because I couldn't conjure love for other people. It wasn't in me. Yet Teresa said, "You will become known as a man of such incredible love that it will become a hallmark of your life." At the time Teresa said those words to me, it was inconceivable to me that it could ever come to pass. There was nothing in my natural condition that would have permitted it. In my tears at that moment I truly was standing at the borders of impossibility. As far as I could or was willing to believe, such a thing just wasn't going to happen.

I now believe that it was God who put those words in Teresa's mouth, and I believe that God has me well on my way to becoming known as a man of compassion and love. It is happening because I made the choice to pray and believe that what seemed impossible to me was not impossible for God. I believe that if I ask according to His will, I will receive. And I believe that it is God's will that His love for people be made manifest in my life. Because I now believe that with all my heart, I am not afraid to ask for it. I'm not afraid to let Him lead me across the border into the land of impossibility—the land He wants me to inherit.

I recall that as a young believer, only saved for a couple of years, I really, really wanted to walk with God but was finding it difficult. Driving my police car one night on Carling Avenue in Ottawa, I was overcome with frustration that I couldn't seem to love people and want them to know Christ. I would talk to people about Jesus, but there was always hollowness inside me where love for the other person should have been. I punched the steering wheel and said aloud, "I'm going to serve You, Jesus, if it kills me."

———

It's hopeless to love others with a sacrificial love if we are not abiding in Christ. We don't have the ability to love others as God loves us on our own volition. Our fleshly nature is not others-centered, nor does it have the capacity to sacrifice our own well-being for the benefit of another. To love other people the way that the Lord commands us to do requires another nature apart from our flesh—it requires the Lord's nature living in and through us. Simply put, we need to open our hearts and say, "Lord, You need to do through me what I cannot do on my own—help me to love others the way You love me."

There are a lot of things you can do in the natural. There are certain behaviors that you can alter. There are certain sins or habits that you have walked away from legitimately before you even became a Christian. However, there are many things about us and in us that we cannot change without the power of God working in us. We cannot love the way Christ loves us in our natural state. It is impossible—I can't do it; you can't do it. It can only come by way of Christ in us. There has to be newness of life and God's nature flowing in and through us.

"This is My commandment, that you love one another as I have loved you. Greater love has no one than this, than to lay down one's life for his friends" (John 15:12–13). It's easy to say, but it's hard to live it out. It's hard to love people who don't reciprocate it. It's hard to love the person that you know is speaking about you behind your back. But God loved us when we were yet separated from Him. He loved us even when we were rebelling against Him. He loved us and showed mercy when we sinned right and left with little or no remorse. In all of this, the Lord poured His grace and mercy upon us and brought us into a relationship with Himself. In the same way, we are to love others—to extend grace and mercy—even when they are our enemies. It's hard to be given to others, especially those who mistreat us or don't like us, but it's a command of God and something that God will enable us to do if we open our hearts to Him and abide in Him. If we don't obey this command, we move to an absence of joy. We move into a religiousness that becomes cold because ultimately Christianity is about God giving Himself for us.

We need to remember that we are ambassadors of the heart of God—in the church first, and secondary to the world. We are the Lord's representatives—witnesses that Christ gave Himself on the cross to redeem each and every person we meet. And our love for one another is to be a sign to the world that we truly are of another spirit!

So how do we, in practical terms, learn to love others as Christ loves us?

John 11:3–6 says, "Therefore the sisters sent to Him, saying, 'Lord, behold, he whom You love is sick.' When Jesus heard that, He said, 'This sickness is not unto death, but for the glory of God, that the Son of God may be glorified through it.' Now Jesus loved Martha and her sister and Lazarus. So, when He heard that he was sick, He stayed two more days in the place where He was."

At first glance you may stop and think, "But I thought Jesus loved them—why would He not rush to help?" In fact, maybe you have asked that question many times regarding your own life. Why aren't You answering my prayers, Lord? Why is my situation still the same? Where are You, Lord? I need You *now*!

God's love is agape love—it's a love that gives people what God knows is necessary in the situation and brings about God's greater purpose and His glory. In this situation with Lazarus, Jesus did not tarry because He didn't love him or care that he would die. Jesus waited because there was a higher purpose at work—the glorifying of God and the witness to all those around that He was the Messiah, the very Redeemer for whom they had so desperately been looking to come for decades. Now, that's amazing! Lazarus had to die for the glory of God to be revealed in and through his life and for his ears to actually be open. When we love people the way God loves us, we have a deep inner trust in God that no matter what they are going through, the Lord is in control of the situation and will be glorified.

Agape love moves us to treat people with understanding and compassion, not compulsion. If I love you, there's a time to speak, and there's a time to be silent. There's a time to have an opinion; there's a time to say nothing. There's a time to let the Holy Spirit say, "The door is not open; don't speak in this situation."

There's a death at work here. I am taking this person to a place, and in that place it is going to look hopeless. And everyone around him or her is going to think it looks hopeless. Then, at the appropriate time, when all else has failed and everybody has lost hope, God is going to give you a word, and you are going to speak that word. Your son or daughter is going to come out of the grave and walk toward the voice of God being spoken through you, and you will see his or her hands raised in the air—you just need to trust God's greater purpose in this situation!

We need to trust God with those we love by putting them into His hands, entrusting them to Him, no matter what it looks like to our eyes, no matter what we hear with our ears, no matter what any voice around us is saying. When we love people the way God loves us, we are able to place them in His loving hands, believing that God will call these people at the appropriate time out of the grave of their experience. True love—God's love working in and through us—has this ability.

To love others as Christ loves us is to let people be close to you. God's love is not a surface feeling or detached from our deepest concerns and thoughts—He draws us in close and knows us intimately—every thought, every fear, every single detail that makes us who we are!

The key to loving others as Christ loved us is making it our deepest inner passion to *love God*. That's where it all begins. We need to love the Lord with all of our heart. The heart is the very essence of my inner passion, my pursuit, why I exist, where I am moving to, and what I am doing. It's the very essence of who I am as a person, and the most important commandment of God is that I am to love Him with this inner passion. My primary pursuit is to be of God. We see this throughout the psalms when David says, "As the deer pants for the water brooks, so pants my soul for You, O God" (Ps. 42:1). David acknowledges that God is the chief pursuit of his heart. When God is your main pursuit—your primary purpose—you want to know Him, walk with Him, and do His will. The first of the greatest commandments is declaring to us that our lives need to be intertwined with God.

In other words, the totality of my life is directed to loving Him, to knowing Him, to understanding Him, and then to allowing Him to work in me so that it begins to flow out through me to all the people who surround me and whom I come into contact with in my daily life.

LOVING OUR NEIGHBOR AS OURSELVES

When you put this all together, it flows as one continual command! It's almost as if Jesus didn't even take a breath between the first and second great commandments. He says the second is like the first, "Thou shalt love thy neighbour as thyself" (Matt. 22:39, KJV). In other words, the ultimate expression of how deeply I love God is reflected in how I interact with other people. First John 4:20 says, "If someone says, 'I love God,' and hates his brother, he is a liar; for he who does not love his brother whom he has seen, how can he love God whom he has not seen?"

I want to make note that the word *hate* in that scripture also has the connotation of indifference. In other words, if a person says, "I love God," but is indifferent to fellow human beings, indifferent to their pain, indifferent to their peril, and indifferent to the difficulty that people without God find themselves in, then the truth is not in him. This person may know the truth, but the truth is not *in* him. People can have a head knowledge of God, but that head knowledge of God has not manifested in their hearts the life (or expression of the life) of the gospel of Christ.

A Christian police officer invited me to go with him into the regional detention center to share Christ with the prisoners. He said that the chief had given permission to go in uniform. It's dangerous enough to go into a prison as a cop. But to go inside wearing the uniform is crazy. I don't mean dropping off a prisoner on duty while in uniform. I mean going into the cellblock behind multiple locked doors and gates where if anything went down, nobody could possibly get there in time to help us. It's a deliberately slow and difficult process getting inside a prison cellblock because people deliberately want it to be hard to get out.

To make matters worse, there had been a violent disturbance in that facility about a month earlier. "If that happens again while we're inside, Bob, we're finished," I said, as if he couldn't figure that out for himself. "There will be no getting out of there alive."

"I know," he confirmed. "Are you coming or not?"

Now my idle boast was being put to the test. Did I love these men enough to go to them despite the danger? Did I love these men enough to be vulnerable before them? Did I love these men enough to put my life in jeopardy for the salvation of their souls? Did I love these men enough to take such a risk to tell them about Jesus Christ? It wasn't a feeling in my heart as much as a conscious and deliberate decision that I needed to do this if I was going to mature in my faith and grow in the Lord. As fearful as it was, I needed to face my fears.

That night I met Bob at the police station, and we drove to the prison, in uniform. On the way Bob said, "If you don't mind, I want to stop on the way at a halfway house for guys reentering society after doing their time. A friend of mine is celebrating the one-year anniversary of his salvation. It's his one-year spiritual birthday tonight. He's an ex-con biker, a member of the Outlaws."

"There's no way he's saved," I blurted out. "These guys can't get saved. You know what they believe. You know their initiation rites. There is no way these men can be saved."

"Come see for yourself, then," Bob challenged me.

The guy celebrating his first spiritual birthday was everything but what I thought he would be. As I suspected, he had all the trappings of the biker wardrobe. But he had tenderness in his heart such as I had only seen in Christian men such as Irv, the Mounty who led me to the Lord. This ex-biker was quick to shed a tear. He truly loved the Lord. Besides being amazed by this man's spiritual presence, I was more amazed to see fifteen or sixteen ex-cons just like him living in the halfway house.

These guys were heavy-duty ex-criminals. They didn't do hard time for soft offenses. They had committed the most violent crimes, horrible abuses of people and property. Yet they weren't afraid to talk freely about what they had done and how God had forgiven them.

We had come just before they were about to have a time of worship, and they asked us if we wanted to stay and if I would like to share my testimony. Bob was OK with it, and I agreed, secretly thinking that it was safer in the halfway house than it would be deep inside the bowels of the prison. They sang, worshipped, and testified in true praise and thanks-giving. As I watched them, I couldn't help but wonder how these men could become something that all of my police training and social bias had convinced me they could not become.

These guys didn't need to play jailhouse religion anymore because they weren't in jail. There was no status to be gained by playing Christian in the penal system any longer. There was no need to put on a dog and pony show for the Parole Board. That was already behind them. Yet there they were, waving their hands, crying, and glorifying God.

These were free men who only had to stay clean and sober and report to their parole officers on time. Other than that, their lives were their own. Six months in the halfway house, and they were back in society. Yet they chose to use their freedom to worship their Creator. They were being the new creations that God had made them.

"I am honored to be here tonight," I said when it was time for my testimony. "I am taken with what I see here, and I thank God for this experience." Then I sat down. I just couldn't bring myself to share my testimony.

They didn't pressure me. But after the worship time was over, a couple of the guys came up to me and asked if I was filled with the Holy Spirit. I didn't really know what that was yet. I told them what I had been taught and explained that when I received Christ, the Holy Spirit came to me. They nodded their heads and said, "Yes, but there is a second touch of God that He wants to give you to give you power to live as a Christian."

I had not been where these guys had been. I wasn't the friendliest, nicest, most loving person on the planet, but I had never lived in the hellhole these guys had spent years in, and I certainly never did the things that got them locked up to begin with. Nevertheless, these guys were way ahead of me in Christ's victory and in serving God.

"Do you know the full power of God?" they asked me, wiping tears from their faces. The toughest criminals you could picture were teary-eyed as they spoke of what the Lord had done in their lives and what He could do in my life. The whole thing was upside down and inside out if you looked at it through natural eyes. I hadn't gone as deep as they had gone in crime, nor had I gone as deep as they had gone in Christ. I was stuck in neutral with my own sense of righteousness, which was quickly fading.

"Would you let us pray for you?" they asked. I agreed. They laid hands on me, which made me extremely nervous. But I allowed it, although I asked the man standing behind me to move.

"Are you sure you don't want me behind you?" he asked, as if he knew something I didn't. He seemed aware of the fact that I might be nervous having a tough ex-con standing directly behind a uniformed officer, but he was also aware that I wasn't aware of what was coming.

"I'm sure I don't want you standing behind me," I told him.

"OK," he said as he moved to the side. The tone in his voice clearly confirmed that he knew something I didn't know. But to my mind, there was nothing strange or unusual about a simple prayer.

God had other things in mind, which included humbling a proud Carter Conlon. They began to pray, everyone speaking at the same time, and I began to lift my hands. I say "began to lift my hands" because I was flat on my back before my arms were fully extended.

I'm not a big believer in the Charismatic stuff around pushing people down while anointing them with oil. The halfway house crowd didn't do any of that. God Himself put me on the floor—on my back, in full uniform, staring at the ceiling, and speaking in tongues. One of the greatest evidences of the Holy Spirit in that moment, besides the fact that I was speaking in tongues, was that I did not care what position I was in. I was totally humbled before God and before men. All of my pride was gone, the uniform meant nothing, ex-cons were singing and rejoicing all around me, I was flat on my back speaking in tongues, and I did not care who knew or who saw.

———✦———

The ultimate expression of how deeply I really do love God is based on how I interact with other people. In other words, the Scripture says that in fact I am to love my neighbor as myself. Who is my neighbor? You may not like the answer, but your neighbor is not just the people you like—your neighbor includes the person that you don't like; the person that you have nothing in common with; the person that sees things completely different than you do; the person that is of a different culture, ethnicity, or belief system; the person that you fear; the person that you stereotype; the person that you disrespect; the person that you consider your mortal enemy!

In Mark 9 Jesus comes down the Mount of Transfiguration to find the father distraught about his child's demon possession, as well as the disciples' lack of power, and this needy father becomes the Lord's immediate neighbor. This man had been beaten up emotionally by the devil, who had taken control of his son's life. He needed Jesus' help in an impossible situation. Jesus could have walked away, as the priest and Levite did when they ignored the plight of a man robbed, beaten, and left half dead by thieves. But a compassionate Samaritan man took pity on the man and transported him to an inn to be cared for: "But a Samaritan, as he traveled, came where the man was; and when he saw him, he took pity on him" (Luke 10:33, NIV). The word *pity* here literally means to be sick to the stomach.

This poor father had been ignored by the religious leaders and sadly found the disciples were unable to help, though they tried (Mark 9:22). So this father, moved to the deepest core of his being, asked Jesus to set his son free. Jesus, like the Good Samaritan, didn't turn away from His neighbor but directly and personally ministered to this father, who was desperate for God's help.

When you love your neighbor as yourself, you are treating them the way you want to be treated. We all want people to love us, to show mercy and grace when we blow it, and we want to be treated with consideration and compassion. But I believe there is something deeper to this as well that many people genuinely struggle with: "How do I love people if I don't love myself?"

For some, it may seem that it is a given that we all love ourselves or think highly of how we should be treated. And though all people want to be treated in a loving and right way, not all people look in the mirror and are pleased with what they see.

Paul the apostle, even in describing the marriage relationship, said that if a man loves his wife, he loves himself. There is something about this that I need to understand.

There are many individuals who are afraid of people. Maybe you are one of them. Maybe you are saying, "I love God—I can seemingly open the Bible and read it. I can come into the prayer closet, but when it comes to people, I have a hard time. I have been so wounded by people that I don't trust them let alone love them!"

The underlying problem that keeps us from loving others is that we fear that God sees us the way we see ourselves. It's the fear that the way I see myself in the mirror, the way I feel about myself—the way that I am aware of all my frailties and failings—is exactly how God sees me. And this fear keeps people out of the prayer closet. It keeps their relationship with God somewhat at a distance because all they see is how far they have fallen short of the glory of God.

My dear friend, if this is something that you grapple with, I have good news for you that will set you free. First John 4:19 says, "We love Him because He first loved us." Before you knew God, He loved you. God knew you before you were formed in your mother's womb. You were not an accident. You were not some fluke of nature or some illegitimate relationship—you were allowed by God to be born. He allowed your mother to conceive—knowing that that person who was going to come forth from the womb was going to be you. And He did it because He loved you. He had a purpose and a plan for your life—something He was going to do in and through you.

In the Old Testament book of Ezekiel, God speaks about His own people of Israel. Chapter 16 verses 5–6 say, "No eye pitied you, to do any of these things for you, to have compassion on you; but you were thrown out into the open field, when you yourself were loathed on the day you were born. And when I passed by you and saw you struggling in your own blood, I said to you in your blood, 'Live!' Yes, I said to you in your blood, 'Live!'"

In other words, God saw you when you were in a terrible condition and everybody passed you by. No one had compassion on you. You were cast out and loathing the day you were born. *But* God said, "I saw you." He saw the potential in your life—He was the only One who saw what you were going to be—not what you were. That is the sinful condition in which you and I were born into this world; without Christ there is nobody here who would have any hope for the future. Our songs would be empty songs, and our hope for eternity would be in vain. *But* God had His eye upon us from the very moment of creation. In verse 6 another translation says, "I saw that thou wast trodden under foot" (DRA). When God saw that you had no hope, He reached down to you and said, "Live."

God saw us in our hopeless, sinful condition. He sent His Son so that we could be redeemed from our sinful nature and be restored to God and to one another! The Bible tells us that "if any man be in Christ, he is a new creature: old things are passed away; behold, all things are become new" (KJV). When Jesus saw you—when you trusted in Him for your salvation—He spoke into your heart and gave you the power to be a different person than the person you once were. God loved you when no one else did. God saw you when no one else could. And God cleansed you when no one else would.

The Lord came down and gave His life on the cross so that all our filth and iniquity that we were born into could be washed away. First John 4:9–10 says, "In this was manifested the love of God toward us, because that God sent his only begotten Son into the world, that we might live through him. Herein is love, not that we loved God, but that he loved us, and sent his Son to be the propitiation for our sins" (KJV).

Our old nature, the one where no good thing exists, was crucified with Christ on the cross. You now have a new nature re-created in Christ to the glory and to the image of the almighty God. The moment you came to Christ, you were born again, re-created into the image of His Son. It is this new nature that you are to love—the new nature of Christ within you—because you love what God is doing in remaking you into His image!

Ironically, as we do this, we find ourselves walking closer to God and our love for God increasing. This then spills into the lives around us, and we find ourselves pouring a kind word and hope into somebody's heart. As we pour love into others, we find that God is increasingly pouring His love into us! Jeremiah 29:11 says, "For I know the thoughts that I think toward you, says the LORD, thoughts of peace and not of evil, to give you a future and a hope."

When I see a downtrodden person on the side of the road, I don't have to know the whole Bible—I just have to know that God loves him the way He loves me.

Love your neighbor as yourself. When you understand how much God loves you—right from the beginning of your life—then you are able to show that same love to everyone you encounter. That means you see each person as God sees you. That means you accept each person as God has accepted you. That means you encourage and build up each person as God has encouraged you and built you up.

The Joy of Serving Others

Joy will fill your heart when you start serving others and love them with the love of Christ. Not only will the Lord give you the ability and the power to love others; He will change how you see people—He will give you fresh eyes and His thoughts so that even your enemies become people you deeply care for and love. It is in this unconditional giving of yourself to other people that you find the diminishing of your own selfish desires and a true foundation of joy welling up in your soul. The Bible tells us that Jesus went to the cross willingly, enduring it and despising the shame, for the joy that was set before Him. Now the Lord sits at the right hand of all authority—and offers you the joy and peace that comes from Him.

Remember, "The weapons we fight with are not the weapons of the world. On the contrary, they have divine power to demolish strongholds. We demolish arguments and every pretension that sets itself up against the knowledge of God, and we take captive every thought to make it obedient to Christ" (2 Cor. 10:4–5, NIV). Only when you are willing to first fight the battle of the mind—where the enemy plants his seeds of disappointment—will you be free to love your neighbor as yourself.

Win the battle of the heart, and you will win the war against the fear of living for others. In our Mark 9 Bible passage, once the father's heart was touched and the disappointments erased by Christ, he could ask in faith for the deliverance of his child (Mark 9:22).

We can't share truth about God's love with any shred of authenticity until we truly begin living for others—until we begin praying for a heart that loves and serves others, just as God has loved and poured out His life for us.

When we pour our lives out for others, we come into the full joy of the gospel.

Joseph's life was more than a promise, a pretty coat, and a palace. There was a pit, a Potiphar, and a prison along the way. Yet going through those doors eventually led Joseph to serve others. He matured into an others-focused man. When he was still in his pretty-coat stage, he was obsessed with himself. But he grew into a generous man, obsessed with providing for others, even though some were not kind to him. It didn't matter if his brothers had changed, because God had changed Joseph!

Although we are all born, without exception, selfish and self-focused to the core of our beings, God will set doors before us that, if we pray and believe enough to pass through, will lead us to a joyous and blessed life of service to others.

Love God and love your neighbor as yourself—there is no greater commandment.

———

I was invited to speak at a Pentecostal church in Ottawa in 2012. At a dinner following the service, a man walked up to me and asked, "Do you remember me?"

I looked into the face of that former biker after more than thirty years, smiled, and said, "Of course I remember you, Brian. What are you doing now?"

"I'm an elder in this church," he said with a broad smile. After serving his prison term and living in the halfway house,

he became a cake decorator. The irony of the transformation from Outlaw biker to cake decorator was not lost on me. Perhaps an even greater irony is that those ex-bikers at the halfway house over thirty years before cared more about me than I cared about them.

The lesson Brian Bloomfield taught me once again was don't limit God. The Lord can save anybody. He can change anybody and anything. In the eyes of the natural world, I was supposed to be the virtuous and righteous man, a Christian dedicated to enforcing the law and protecting the public. But God had done something in those public enemies, through their pain, that He did for me by simply inviting me to pass through an open door. I didn't understand it at all at the time. But what God really needs is a church that cares for His children the way those ex-criminals cared for me.

IMPORTANT TAKEAWAYS FROM THIS CHAPTER

KEY THOUGHT: Win the battle of the heart, and you will win the war against fear of living for others.

KEY WORD: Compassion

KEY INSIGHT: Loving your neighbor as yourself

Chapter Five

PRAYING FOR THE IMPOSSIBLE

D O YOU BELIEVE that God can do the impossible in your life? I mean, *really* believe?

I read a little story once that I want to share with you here:

Robert Dick Wilson was one of the great professors at Princeton Theological Seminary. One of his students had been invited to preach in Miller Chapel twelve years after his graduation. Old Dr. Wilson came in and sat down near the front. At the close of the meeting, the old professor came up to his former student, cocked his head to one side in his characteristic way, extended his hand, and said, "If you come back again, I will not come to hear you preach. I only come once. I am glad that you are a big-godder. When my boys come back, I come to see if they are big-godders or little-godders, and then I know what their ministry will be." His former student asked him to explain, and he replied, "Well, some men have a little God, and they are always in trouble with him. He can't do any miracles. He can't take care of the inspiration and transmission of the Scripture to us. He doesn't intervene on behalf of his people. They have a little God and I call them little-godders. Then, there are those who have a great God. He speaks and it is done. He commands and it stands fast. He knows how to show himself strong on behalf of them that fear him. You have a great God; and he will bless your ministry." He paused a moment, smiled, said, "God bless you," and turned and walked out.[1]

What about you? Are you a little-godder or a big-godder?

Throughout the history of humanity, God's people time and again have found themselves facing the impossible. And time and again, the Lord showed Himself strong on behalf of His people.

In our present age, however, it would seem that the church has fallen spiritually asleep. We have become little-godders and have found ourselves inwardly confused and outwardly defeated, all because we have focused on the natural and have stepped back from the true work of God.

The Christian life is not lived in the natural, yet that's exactly what so many believers are trying to do—and that includes leadership in many churches as well. We have moved away from the supernatural walk of the Holy Spirit and have relied on ingenuity, programs, and professional skills to try to accomplish God's work. We have moved from the compassion of God that was exhibited on the cross to an inward focus.

Is it any wonder that we seem so weak and ineffective—in our own lives and in our communities and nation?

The Scriptures are replete with examples and admonitions of walking in the Spirit rather than the flesh. Yet many in this church age don't believe or rely on the Holy Spirit and have therefore limited themselves (and God) to the possible as humans conceive it.

Our lack of prayer and faith has brought about a church body that lives in the natural and the possible, despite exhaustive historical records and eyewitness testimonials of how God operates in a supernatural world of impossibility. Throughout history God has taken people with little apparent or actual skill and used them to accomplish supernatural things.

God called Gideon a "man of valor" (Judg. 6:12). No human being would have referred to Gideon that way at the time God called him into service. The word *valor* in the original text means man of incredible resource. Gideon, looking at his own natural circumstances, complained that his father was of the least tribe in Israel and his family was the least of the least tribe. Gideon completed the hat trick by describing himself as the least in his father's house. Yet, even as Gideon protested to God that he, Gideon, had limited resources, God replied, "I've given you My word. That's all you need."

What was true for Gideon is true for us today!

God has given us the power of His Word and His Holy Spirit to live our Christian walk and accomplish His will. Where God says He is able to take you, what He says He is able to do, wherever He has determined to lead you is entirely possible as long as God Himself is the author and finisher of it. Your part is prayer and faith. Anything other than that, once you get involved, will tarnish the Word of God or take something that should glorify the name of Christ and diminish it.

Jesus' growth strategy for the church is found in Acts 1:7–8, which says, "He said to them, 'It is not for you to know times or epochs which the Father has fixed by His own authority; but you will receive power when the Holy Spirit has come upon you; and you shall be My witnesses both in Jerusalem, and in all Judea and Samaria, and even to the remotest part of the earth'" (NASB).

———•◦•———

Years ago we were in Jamaica for a three-day evangelistic crusade in an area of the inner city of Kingston. This particular area had been given over to violence and mayhem for thirty years. The population was tens of thousands, and unemployment was extremely high. Six drug lords controlled the whole area and constantly vied for supremacy in the drug trade.

It got so violent in this community that the government plowed down a thirty-acre field between the six areas that were under the control of the drug lords. That area became known as "no-man's land."

An unwritten law was created that no person was allowed to cross that land to the other side. It was a buffer zone. Anybody who tried to cross was usually shot at by people from the other side. Over the span of thirty years there were over eight hundred murders recorded on that infamous field. Those were the recorded ones, but people told us there were a lot more murders than eight hundred.

The Lord called us to set up a platform in this no-man's land and have a three-day crusade!

He spoke to my heart that He was about to destroy the power of violence, poverty, and unemployment and was going to do a miracle in this sin-ravaged community.

I remember gathering the pastors together from the community and telling them what the Lord had spoken. I told them God had spoken something to my heart and that I fully believed it was going to happen. I let them know that there was going to be a revival in this area, that thousands of people were going to be saved and that they were going to have to be there and be ready to disciple these people.

I remember them looking at me, and more than one got up and walked out of the meeting. They said I was a madman!

"It's crazy—it's a dangerous area to go in, and people don't go there," they said.

Just before we set up the crusade, we had to hire a mercenary soldier, who was feared by all those in the area. He actually was a very tough guy. In order for us to hold the crusade in that area, we had to get permission from all six drug lords, or they could kill us.

There was no law there anymore. The government had tried to disarm the rebels and the warlords after the attacks in NYC on 9/11, but they failed in their efforts.

While I was riding in the car with the tough soldier, he looked at me and said, "You guys are nuts; you are completely nuts. Nobody is coming to this thing. In fact, you will be lucky if you don't get yourselves killed. You have no idea what you are dealing with."

We set up the stage on the field. There was only a little flock of Christian people, but because of fear some wouldn't come on the field. So the people on the periphery of this thirty-acre parcel of land were about five or six rows deep—but no matter what, they wouldn't come onto the field.

As I was speaking on Ezekiel 37, the Holy Spirit came on me, and I stood back and forgot for a moment where I was, but I leaned over the pulpit, and I began to cry for the people. I wept and cried out, "Oh, Holy Spirit, come." It was a moment in which I realized that all was hopeless apart from the Holy Spirit! I just kept asking the Spirit to breathe on these dear people so that they may live.

I didn't care what people thought as they saw me crying out. It didn't matter because I knew the hopelessness of the moment if God didn't intervene. The weeping that had come on me suddenly hit the front row of the people and just started going down the line! One of the concessionaires who was way at the back of this field told me later that the thug (one of the drug lord's minions—and there were many) who was standing next to her started to weep as well. Before I knew it, people started to fill the field!

That night about two thousand people met me at the altar and came to Christ. It was an amazing night! By the last night of the crusade, there were fourteen thousand people on that field. Many came to Christ, and the spirit of violence was broken.

On that field today the government has built beautiful houses and condominiums. What used to be no-man's land now holds a church and a children's playground. The Queen of England found out what was happening and donated personal money to build a pottery-making plant. Now there is employment and a thriving community, all because God did the impossible!

————⋙⋘————

"The spirit shrieked, convulsed him violently and came out. The boy looked so much like a corpse that many said, 'He's dead.' But Jesus took him by the hand and lifted him to his feet, and he stood up" (Mark 9:26–27, NIV).

When God is at work in a person's life or in a community, the end result does not always look like what we expected. But when it is God at work, the impossible gets answered and the fruit of the miracle continues.

When Jesus came down the Mount of Transfiguration, the crowd came running to Him. They wanted to see a miracle. It was then that the demonic spirit manifested itself before them (v. 20). This is how the enemy works. He manifests his power before God does His work in order to put fear and doubt into your mind and to stop you from trusting God. I've seen it happen so many times, and because of that I have learned when the enemy shows his hand, it's because God is about to do something amazing! I'm sure when the crowd suddenly saw the boy writhing in agony on the ground and foaming at the mouth, they were filled with fear and thought it was an impossible situation.

Even after Jesus cast the demon out, the initial result looked no different from what had already been witnessed—in fact, it looked much worse. The boy was cast to the ground again, but this time it looked as though he were dead (v. 26). Had the power of God been unable to counter the power of Satan?

Was Jesus no better than His disciples who could not cast the demon out? It sure seemed like it.

Imagine how confusing (and disappointing) this must have been for the father.

Over the years I have heard sincere people make this statement: "Every time I get serious about the Lord and make a decision to live fully for Him, I get severely attacked. At times I have thought it's easier not to be a Christian than be one and open myself up to this attack."

I imagine this was the sentiment of the crowd as they watched the boy writhing on the ground. They must have thought it would have been better for the child to remain "possessed" and alive than to be "delivered" and dead.

Beloved, this is exactly what the enemy wants you to believe. People give up at the very point of true victory. Jesus wasn't finished yet. When the devil is cast out, like he was at our crusade in Jamaica, that's only the beginning of the miracle. It's what follows that counts.

The very next moment Jesus reached down and took the child by the hand and lifted him up; immediately life began to flow into the boy. The Greek text literally means to awaken. What looks like death to us is nothing more than sleep to God. I'm sure when the boy stood up, the father and the crowd of onlookers were amazed! Life came to the child that day, and he would go on to live a life like everyone else, neither marginalized nor impaired by what the devil had done in the past. Jesus had done the impossible.

Do you find yourself in an impossible place right now?

You are not alone. This is exactly what confronted the prophet Ezekiel.

The Scriptures tell us God had taken Ezekiel by the Spirit to a dry valley that was strewn with dead people's bones—as far as the eye could see, there was nothing but death.

Read the following Scripture passage in Ezekiel 37:1–10:

> The hand of the LORD came upon me and brought me out in the Spirit of the LORD, and set me down in the midst of the valley; and it was full of bones. Then He caused me to pass by them all around, and behold, there were very many in the open valley; and indeed they were very dry. And He said to me, "Son of man, can these bones live?"
>
> So I answered, "O Lord GOD, You know."
>
> Again He said to me, "Prophesy to these bones, and say to them, 'O dry bones, hear the word of the LORD! Thus says the Lord GOD to these bones: "Surely I will cause breath to enter into you, and you shall live. I will put sinews on you and bring flesh upon you, cover you with skin and put breath in you; and you shall live. Then you shall know that I am the LORD."'"
>
> So I prophesied as I was commanded; and as I prophesied, there was a noise, and suddenly a rattling; and the bones came together, bone to bone. Indeed, as I looked, the sinews and the flesh came upon them, and the skin covered them over; but there was no breath in them.
>
> Also He said to me, "Prophesy to the breath, prophesy, son of man, and say to the breath, 'Thus says the Lord GOD: "Come from the four winds, O breath, and breathe on these slain, that they may live."'" So I prophesied as He commanded me, and breath came into them, and they lived, and stood upon their feet, an exceedingly great army.

The same words that God spoke to Ezekiel and the nation of Israel He is speaking to us today. It says that the hand of the Lord came upon Ezekiel and, through the power of the

Spirit, took him to a huge valley—an open valley—filled with dead men's bones. Little did Ezekiel know at the time that he was going to see a tremendous miracle of the Lord. The first thing you need to see in this passage is that before Ezekiel could see the impossible become possible, he needed the Spirit of the Lord on him.

The hand of the Lord came upon him, and the power of the Spirit led him.

You will never rely on the supernatural until the natural ends. In other words, until you come to the end of yourself—your skills, your schemes, and your manipulation of circumstances—you will not experience the power of God working out the impossible in your life.

We need to be filled with the Holy Spirit—relying on (trusting) God's Word and communicating with Him through prayer—rather than trying to live out our faith in the natural.

The Lord does not withhold His Spirit from us—He wants to work in and through our lives, but too often we forfeit His hand upon us because we are dead to prayer, dead to His Word, and lacking in faith!

Prayer to a Christian is the very breath of life, and God's Word is our sustenance. When we forsake both of these vital components, we are left with living in the natural, which never brings about God's power and redemptive work.

The hand of the Lord came upon him, and the power of the Spirit led him.

I want you to look at your life right now. Are you facing an impossible situation? Is the Lord working in and through you to bring about His desired end?

Can you say this? The hand of the Lord came upon (your name), and the power of the Spirit led (your name).

When you put your name in place of "him," does it speak

the truth over your life right now? If it doesn't, do you want the hand of the Lord upon you? Do you want the power of the Spirit leading you? If the answer is yes, then rejoice and start asking God to come upon you and to lead you by the power of His Holy Spirit. That's a prayer that the Lord gladly answers because He wants all of us to walk daily in the truth, wisdom, and power of His Spirit!

By the power of the Lord's Spirit, Ezekiel was led out into this vast wasteland—a huge, open valley that was filled with the bones of the dead. The word *open* in that context means that there was lifelessness on their faces. The dead bones refer to the people of Israel who had turned their backs on God. There was no sense of expectancy for their future; instead, they were opened to the display of their own powerlessness. We need to understand that these were religious people who did not set out to be spiritually dead. They didn't set out to be immoral, nor did they plan on dying around the altars they built.

But that's exactly what happened.

Ezekiel is told by the Lord how dry and arid the bones are in this valley. The word *dry* in this passage means sterile. In other words, God's people were incapable of producing life. And this is where many Christians live today.

If we are going to become what God would have us to be, we have to get to the point of agreeing with God concerning where we are spiritually. We have got to come to that place where we finally just agree with God that we are living in the natural instead of in the Spirit and stop making excuses for our lack of strength, our lack of influence, and our lack of bringing life to our homes and communities because we lack the outworking of the Holy Spirit. One hundred twenty people in the early church were able to change the world through the gospel because they were empowered by God's Spirit. Today we have 120 churches in close proximity in one community, and we can't make an impact! Why? Because too many of us are like the dead man's bones in the valley—lacking strength, influence, and life—due to the fact that we are walking in the natural instead of in the Spirit.

You see, at some point there has to be an honest evaluation of the heart. We can't be afraid of that. You can't be afraid of it, and I can't be afraid of it. David, the king of Israel, cried out, "Search me, O God, and know my heart; try me, and know my ways. And if there is something in me that isn't right, God, lead me in the paths of life." (See Psalm 139:23–24.) That was the cry of his heart. And that needs to be the cry of your heart, my heart, and every Christian's heart. "Lord, put Your hand upon me. Lead me by Your Spirit. I find myself in an impossible place. I can barely get up in the morning, and though I want to live for You, I am not making it on my own. Lord, fill me with Your Spirit so I can honor You, bear good fruit, and see You do the impossible in my world."

As the Lord led Ezekiel through the valley and showed him the multitude of dry bones, He then asked, "Can these bones live, Ezekiel?"

It takes absolutely no faith to say *no* to that question. Anybody can live on the side of unbelief. You don't have to know the Scripture, and you don't have to have any strength of character. It's easy to reply, "It can't be done!" God's question would be considered impossible in the natural. These aren't people who just passed away. These are dry bones that have separated from each other over a span of many, many years. In other words, it was absolutely impossible that these bones could once again become living people—at least in the natural.

Ezekiel responds by saying, "O Lord GOD, You know."

Ezekiel didn't say no. He recognized that the impossibility from his perspective was certainly possible from God's perspective.

When we realize that we are at the end of ourselves and what we can do, we start to recognize that God's perspective is very different. I truly believe that the Lord leads us into impossible situations to open our eyes to the fact that we can't live our lives on our own—that we need Him and His Spirit to work in and through us.

The Lord said to Ezekiel, "Prophesy to these bones, and say to them, 'O dry bones, hear the word of the LORD!'" These bones represent people whose hope is gone. They are cut off from the promises that were once theirs. They have failed God. Yet in the midst of all of this, the Lord's grace is profound, and He tells Ezekiel to speak to them, which in the original language is translated as "sing."

Imagine that—the Lord isn't telling Ezekiel to yell at them but to sing to them. The Lord was moved with compassion and mercy toward His people. So often we assume that the Lord is angry with us when we fail. But just as a father disciplines his child, so the Lord loves His people and desires to redeem them!

"Then said he unto me, Prophesy unto the wind, prophesy, son of man, and say to the wind, Thus saith the Lord GOD; Come from the four winds, O breath, and breathe upon these slain, that they may live" (Ezek. 37:9, KJV).

Right before Ezekiel's eyes the Lord began His work of redemption, and the dry bones came together—the sinew, the organs, and the flesh were brought back together by the power of the Spirit of God. The impossible became possible. That which was dead was made alive. The Lord did what He loves to do—He redeemed the people, He redeemed the nation, He redeemed the arid situation, and He redeemed the outcome of death with His life.

Are you in a dry and arid place? Is the "impossible" set before you? Speak with faith toward Christ concerning every word that has come from His lips to you, and claim the full victory—the four winds. In other words, cry out to the Lord and say, "Surround me, O God; surround me with what You say about my life and my future, and cause me to live. Lord, don't let any other voice hit me from any side but Yours."

Call to the voice of God, and ask Him to speak into your life and drive out the fear, doubt, and unbelief that rule in your heart. God is still the God of the impossible. His promises are real and still as true today as they were in the day of Ezekiel.

I was leading a prayer meeting in a home associated with our little Riceville, Canada, church when someone came in and interrupted us. "It's your wife," the person said. "She says it's an emergency and she needs to speak to you right away." I excused myself and went to the telephone.

"What do you need me to do?" I asked Teresa.

"David Wilkerson called, and he wants you to speak in New York City next Tuesday night."

"Stop fooling around," I said impatiently. "I'm leading a prayer meeting."

"David Wilkerson called, and he wants you to speak in New York City next Tuesday night," she repeated in her "I'm not joking" voice.

"Well," I said, haltingly, "did you tell him I would pray about it?"

"No," Teresa said matter-of-factly. "I told him you would be there."

We laugh about it now, but Teresa's resolve wasn't without some warning and precedent. I did pray about it and found that my spirit agreed with her. We didn't see that telephone call coming. But looking back, the signs were all there.

It turns out that Pastor Dave was driving home from Pennsylvania to New York, listening to one of my messages on tape, when the Lord told him to call me. May 19, 1994, the day David Wilkerson called our house in Riceville, was his sixty-third birthday.

"Did he mention the name of the message he heard?" I asked Teresa while we were still on the telephone discussing Pastor Dave's invitation.

"When a Prayer Becomes a Cry," she said.

That was the message I preached in 1990 when the Lord kept speaking the name David Wilkerson to me. It was now 1994. I immediately knew there was a divine connection, and the moment she heard Pastor Dave's voice on the telephone from New York City, Teresa did too. At that time I didn't know the extent or the details of the connection. As far as I knew, David Wilkerson simply felt encouraged by the message and wanted his congregation to hear it.

I didn't know in that moment that Leonard Ravenhill had sent that cassette to David Wilkerson and that Pastor Dave had driven around for nearly two years with that cassette in his glove compartment before he pulled it out and listened to it. In fact,

Pastor Dave told me later that he had a glove box full of cassettes and he took them all out to toss them. But for whatever reason, he held on to my cassette and listened to it.

As I arrived in New York City on Tuesday, May 24, 1994, I knew I was entering unfamiliar territory. From a wide spot in the road like Riceville, Ontario, Canada, to the largest city in North America (Mexico City might argue, but you get the point), it was one of the most improbable moves imaginable.

After I preached "When a Prayer Becomes a Cry" in Canada in 1990, I told Teresa, "A funny thing happened to me as I delivered this word today. David Wilkerson kept coming into my mind over and over again." I had never met David Wilkerson, nor had I ever been to New York City. It made no sense at all why I couldn't get his name out of my head.

A year or so after I preached that message in 1990, I received a call from Leonard Ravenhill, who lived in Texas. I didn't know much about Ravenhill except that he was well esteemed in the Christian world and was the author of some powerful books on revival. "I've heard a message of yours," he said. Ravenhill spoke regularly in Canada and had been given a recording of my sermon along the way. "I'd like you to come see me," he continued. So I got on an airplane and flew to Lindale, Texas, and spent three days with Leonard Ravenhill.

For three days he poured his heart into me from seven in the morning until seven at night. The only breaks we took were for lunch and his snooze time every afternoon. During those three days he told me everything he could about his experience in ministry and his knowledge of the Word. At the end of our time together, on the day I was to leave, he sat down on a chair and wept. "I have a word from God for you," he started. "I don't do this very often. But the Lord has spoken to me, and I want to share with you what He said." Leonard Ravenhill then proceeded to describe to me what God had shown him about my future—including many of the things that have now played out in my life and several things that have yet to come—most all of which I have described in this book.

"I am commissioned of the Lord to pray for you every day for the rest of my life," Ravenhill went on. He wrote to me quite often after that to encourage me, and as far as I know, he prayed for me every day until he died in 1994. That conversation, as far as I knew, was the end of our visit. The things Leonard Ravenhill spoke to me and the things I am describing in this book were impossible except for God.

I firmly believed that the call from Ravenhill to go visit him and the call from David Wilkerson to go preach in New York City were calls from God.

After meeting with Leonard Ravenhill, I returned to the church I was pastoring in Canada. God was doing wonderful things there, and I was grateful for that. Other than his letters of encouragement, I didn't give a lot more thought to what Leonard had shared with me. He was a wonderful man of God, and the fact that he was praying for me daily touched me deeply. But I was focused on the work at hand with our rapidly growing ministry in the community we were serving.

Little did I know at the time that the time spent with Ravenhill would reshape the entirety of my future.

———◦•◦———

Zechariah 4:6 says, "Then he answered and spake unto me, saying, This is the word of the LORD unto Zerubbabel, saying, Not by might, nor by power, but by my spirit, saith the LORD of hosts" (KJV).

When we pray for the impossible, that means we recognize that nothing will be accomplished by the natural—our abilities or our own mechanisms—but by God's Spirit. Miracles, for the Christian, should not be something we just accept but expect. Now, in saying that, it doesn't mean that God throws His miracles around like an item that can be found at the dollar store. God's miracles are not for your personal enjoyment or luxury. Yes, God can bless us. But He's not a cosmic genie who hands out cheap miracles for our own selfish benefit. God works in the impossible to bring redemption and to bring glory to His name. God's will is about accomplishing God's work in our lives. That's why some people are healed miraculously from disease and others are not. What will bring about God's greater purpose and glory in our situation? We pray and believe the Lord for the impossible and watch Him bring about that which the natural cannot do.

God declares through the promises in His Word that He is going to take you and make you into something much greater than you are. It's the visible testimony God gives to His church that you and I are made into much more than we could ever hope to be in our own strength. We change by the Spirit of God, Paul says, from image to image and glory to glory.

The changed lives of people, redeemed by the power of the cross, are the greatest witness of the truth of the gospel to our fallen and needy world.

THE LORD'S RAGTAG TEAM THAT TURNED THE WORLD UPSIDE DOWN

There is no doubt that the Lord often chooses the most unlikely people to lead His people. The Bible records time and again how God's leaders and prophets were often not the most attractive, educated, brawny, or qualified for the job—at least not from our natural, human perspective. Scripture tells us that we look on the outward but God looks at the heart.

Jesus' selection of disciples would probably not match up to what a CEO would look for in hiring a leader—especially a leader of a new movement! The Lord doesn't look so much at what we are but rather at what He can mold us into. The apostles were a ragtag team, most of them blue-collar fishermen, with a dreaded tax collector thrown into the mix.

After the death of Jesus on the cross, this motley crew ran to the Upper Room and hid! All of them deserted Christ in His hour of need, all of them were filled with fear, all of them doubted and were ready to walk away, and all of them could be classified as failures. Even after three years of living with the Lord and watching all of His tremendous miracles and seeing the power of God on display, they ran and hid.

When the Lord rose from the grave, did He bypass His disciples? Did He say, "Look, you are all dead; you have made all these boasts, but look at the mess you have made. You could have stood visibly and been a testimony of the power of God, but instead, you all took off and hid"? No, the Lord didn't reject His disciples. And even though they failed, they all stayed huddled together in the Upper Room. The disciples knew that they were weak. They knew that they needed the strength of God.

Listen, if we are bringing something to the table, if we have a measure of pride in our own accomplishments and in our own strength, we will never fully know the power of God. The blessing of the Lord is for those who finally come to the end of themselves and say: "Lord, I just come to You as I am; I come to You in my brokenness and in my hopelessness. I come to You in my failure; I come to You with the mess I have made of my life, and I bring the sum total of this mess to You and trust that You are able to raise it from the dead and bring honor to Your name."

God empowered His apostles through His Spirit to bring the gospel to the world. As time went on, this ragtag team grew into men of God. The more they served as witnesses, the more opposition they faced. Even though they had come a long way, they did not rest on their accomplishments, works, and spiritual growth. When the religious leaders put more pressure on them, commanding them to not speak in Jesus' name, the apostles gathered together and prayed.

In Acts 4:29–33 we read, "'Now, Lord, look on their threats, and grant to Your servants that with all boldness they may speak Your word, by stretching out Your hand to heal, and that signs and wonders may be done through the name of Your holy Servant Jesus.' And when they had prayed, the place where they were assembled together was shaken; and they were all filled with the Holy Spirit, and they spoke the word of God with boldness. Now the multitude of those who believed were of one heart and one soul; neither did anyone say that any of the things he possessed was his own, but they had all things in common. And with great power the apostles gave witness to the resurrection of the Lord Jesus. And great grace was upon them all."

The apostles were as one—they were united in prayer and united in faith. There was no division or one apostle having preeminence over another. They recognized that they all had been called by Christ to be testimonies of the gospel and that the power of God was working in and through them—doing what they could never do in their natural state.

"And with great power the apostles gave witness to the resurrection of the Lord Jesus. And great grace was upon them all."

It doesn't say, "And with great education the apostles gave witness to the resurrection of the Lord Jesus." Nor does it say, "And with great programs the apostles gave witness to the resurrection of the Lord Jesus." The early church did not rely on man-made skills, research, wealth, argument, programs, and so on. The apostles relied on *God's power* and *God's leading*. That's it. And that's more than enough!

By God's power, they were made into what they could never be, folks. They were given what they could never possess, and they were taken where they could never go.

These failures come out of that Upper Room changed by the power of God, every last one of them infused with God's Holy Spirit—infused with the life of God. The Scriptures came to life in their hearts; faith bubbled over like a spring within them, just as Jesus had promised (a river of living water flowing out of them).

Every one of the apostles was given the ability to speak and do things that he couldn't do in the natural.

When the 120 believers came out of that upper room in Jerusalem, truths were flowing out of their mouths mingled with future promises that were impossible to accomplish apart from the power of God. Then at Pentecost, when those 3,000 people looked at the 120, they must have wondered where and how they ever acquired that kind of faith. They all had access to the same Scriptures, and yet here were people coming out of a place of intimacy with God who were speaking of things strange and wonderful in a manner that all knew was supernatural. They were speaking with confidence and conviction about things that the 3,000 couldn't see or imagine. The way the 120 were speaking was so compelling that the 3,000 listening essentially said, "Whatever relationship these people have with God that can produce this kind of excitement, power, and fervor—we want that."

The apostles did not relegate God to the realm of the possible. They got together and prayed and in unison said, "You are God."

That's where our prayer has to start—"You are God! You spoke, and the worlds were created. You spoke, and life came into being. You spoke, and animals were created. You looked at dust in the earth, and You spoke and breathed, and man became a living soul. You are God—nothing is impossible with You."

"All things are possible to him who believes" (Mark 9:23).

———◆◆◆———

New York was an open door that God set before me, and I decided to believe once again that impossibility could become possible. After I arrived in New York, I remember walking down Broadway across the street from Times Square Church with David Wilkerson. We were in front of the Winter Garden Theatre, where the Broadway musical Cats *was playing at the time. That's the moment he asked, "Would you be willing to pray and consider coming to help me here in New York?"*

"Wouldn't you like to hear me preach first?" I asked. It surprised me that I was barely off the airplane when David Wilkerson was asking me to join his staff.

"Oh," he said. "Yes, of course, that would be a good idea."

Pastor Dave wasn't caught by surprise. I could tell by the way he answered my question that he was much farther down the faith road than I was. He was simply caught off guard by the fact that I was still in chapter one when he was already more than halfway through the book. Sure enough, I found out later that he already had a word from God that I was to help him at Times Square Church.

He already knew he wanted me there and had been praying about it a great deal. And God had confirmed it. But when reminded, he slowed down to let me catch up. We agreed it would be better to fulfill the law than to leapfrog over it. So I preached a message that night that God had given me titled "Chasing Darkness With a Stick."

It was a message about God's plan to deliver His people from an evil plot by sending a man who was weak in himself but strong in faith. God's lone warrior had nothing more than confidence that his God would destroy the evil plan. I clearly remember preaching that message on Tuesday, May 24, 1994.

Such is the power of God's word, spoken through His servants. I remember how the joy of the Lord hit me so powerfully that night that I started to leap and dance on the platform. I had rarely done that before, even in my own church. The joy became contagious, and the people rose to their feet and started shouting.

However, I recall how I went from sheer joy to worry in an instant. "That is David Wilkerson standing a few feet away from me on the platform," I thought. "I don't know much about him except that he is known to want powerful themes in messages, and here I am dancing. I'm done here."

When I finished and walked back to my seat beside Pastor Dave, he leaned over to me.

"Uh-oh," I thought. "He's not even going to wait until the curtain comes down. He's going to dismiss me right here during the final song."

"How soon can you come back?" he asked.

In an instant, impossibility became possible in a way that only God can do it. When the curtain did come down, he began speaking to me seriously about coming to New York City to help him.

It was a difficult thing for me to consider in the natural. New York was an unfamiliar environment. It was a new country and a new culture. There were over one hundred nationalities represented at Times Square Church. It occurred to me that I could step on all kinds of toes without being aware of it.

To join David Wilkerson at Times Square Church was a decision that no one would walk into lightly— neither David Wilkerson nor I. I knew, for example, that I was out of my league in New York's Times Square. As far as natural experience went, it was way over my head. Yet I knew even then that the God I serve is the God of the impossible. The God I believe in puts the Gideons on the mountaintop to win the victory. The God I believe in puts the Esthers in front of the kings to liberate their people. The God I believe in still calls fishermen (and cops) and fills them with the Holy Ghost, sending them to confound those who stand in their own wisdom and strength.

I had to determine if I really believed the God I served was the God of the impossible if I was going to take David Wilkerson's offer seriously. I sensed in my heart that if I did not believe this, if I harbored any doubt, I would draw back into a place that I would regret all of my life.

———

Our unbelief does not bring about God's work in our lives. If we continue to be prayerless and faithless, we might as well lay in the open field of dry bones lamenting our powerlessness, lamenting our impossible situations, lamenting our culture, and carrying on with our powerless sermons!

Or we can start to hear the word of the Lord and start praying. We can turn to God and ask for the power of His Spirit to work in and through our lives. Jesus said, "If you then, being evil, know how to give good gifts to your children, how much more will your heavenly Father give the Holy Spirit to those who ask Him!" (Luke 11:13).

The Lord has promised to give you His Holy Spirit—to empower you to be the person that God wants you to be. Without the Holy Spirit there will be no awakening. We have already brought our natural best to the table—we have brought our physical strength, we have brought our natural intellects, and we have brought our best-laid and sincere plans. But none of these things have the power to change us into the image of Christ. None of these things have the power to change the world.

Friend, we don't need a new plan, and we don't need a new superstar; we need the Holy Spirit.

Sometimes it takes a while for the truth or the facts to settle into our heart. For instance, the disciples didn't absorb the statement in Mark 9:19 when Jesus said to them, "You unbelieving generation…how long shall I stay with you? How long shall I put up with you? Bring the boy to me" (NIV).

The truth of the disciples' unbelief had not registered in their minds, so when they were alone with Jesus, they asked why they couldn't cast out the demon. Jesus restates it another way: "This kind can come forth by nothing, but by prayer and fasting" (v. 29, KJV). The day was coming when the disciples would receive the power of the Holy Spirit, who would confirm God's will and His Word to them. They would be brought to a place where they would put their trust in Him even in the face of martyrdom.

It was difficult to uproot and bring my children to New York because they were so entrenched in their communities. They were in good schools. They were in a good church community and had good friends.

I remember being in an apartment looking out over the New York City skyline and realizing that the city didn't appeal to me at all. The only real familiarity I ever had with New York City before that time was from watching The Cross and the Switchblade *with gang members chasing each other through alleys. It had zero appeal in the natural. I remember asking God, "What will happen to my children coming to this city and to this church? What will it do to them? How will they survive in this kind of environment?"*

"Are you willing to trust Me?" God asked me as I gazed out that window. "Are you willing to trust Me with your children? Are you willing to trust Me with your family? Are you willing to trust that I will provide for you?"

That day I put my family in the hands of God and chose to believe all over again that what appeared to be impossible could be possible.

IMPORTANT TAKEAWAYS FROM THIS CHAPTER

KEY THOUGHT: God performs the impossible for those willing to believe Him.

KEY WORD: Trust

KEY INSIGHT: When God puts a word in your heart to believe for the impossible, the Holy Spirit will confirm it to you. You are not alone in your walk of faith for the impossible.

Chapter Six

PRAYING FOR FORGIVENESS

BILLY GRAHAM OFTEN said that 75 percent of patients in hospitals would be made whole if they would only forgive.

Many, many people suffer betrayal, injustice, and maltreatment at the hands of others. Christians are not immune to this—we suffer at the hands of others as well. And the betrayal, injustice, and maltreatment that we suffer can cause us to live in a certain place that brings even more suffering to our lives. When we succumb to the bondage of bitterness and hatred toward those who have hurt or treated us badly, we play into the hands of the enemy and block God's healing and provision from pouring into our lives.

There is a better way to deal with betrayal.

There is a better way to deal with injustice.

There is a better way to deal with maltreatment.

———◆———

John Perkins, in his book Let Justice Roll Down, *tells how Jesus' forgiveness is what enabled him to forgive. This is what he says:*

The Spirit of God worked on me as I lay in that bed. An image formed in my mind. The image of the cross—Christ on the cross. It blotted out everything else in my mind.

This Jesus knew what I had suffered. He understood. And He cared. Because He had experienced it all Himself.

This Jesus, this One who had brought good news directly from God in heaven, had lived what He preached. Yet He was arrested and falsely accused. Like me, He went through an unjust trial. He also faced a lynch mob and got beaten. But even more than that, He was nailed to rough wooden planks and killed. Killed like a common criminal....

But when He looked at the mob that had lynched Him, He didn't hate them. He loved them. He forgave them. And He prayed [to] God to forgive them. "Father, forgive these people, for they don't know what they are doing."

His enemies hated. But Jesus forgave. I couldn't get away from that.

The Spirit of God kept working on me and in me until I could say with Jesus, "I forgive them, too." I promised Him that I would "return good for evil," not evil for evil. And He gave me the love I knew I would need to fulfill His command to me of "love your enemy."...

It's a profound, mysterious truth—Jesus' concept of love overpowering hate. I may not see its victory in my lifetime. But I know it's true.

I know it's true, because it happened to me. On that bed, full of bruises and stitches—God made it true in me. He washed my hatred away and replaced it with a love for the white man in rural Mississippi.

I felt strong again. Stronger than ever. What doesn't destroy me makes me stronger.

I know it's true.
Because it happened to me.[1]

⎯⎯◆⎯◆⎯⎯

We have all been hurt, betrayed, and treated badly by others. Some of us have been abused and brutalized in ways that are hard to comprehend.

God's Word is full of real-life stories of people inflicting pain on others. Throughout the Old and New Testaments we read time and again of betrayal, injustice, brutality, and abuses carried out, often, I might mention, against God's people.

The hurts that we experience are as old as sin entering the world. The very first murder in history happened within the very first human family to walk the earth! Adam and Eve's son Cain killed his brother Abel out of jealousy and hatred.

How are we to respond to those who have hurt and betrayed us?

God's Word tells us that suffering is, in some measure, a doorway to knowing Christ in such a way that we can't know by any other method.

That truth in no way belittles the pain you experience brought on by the actions of another, but it does set into motion the process of freedom from the bondage of hate, bitterness, and hardness of heart that can smother the work of God in your life.

Most of us will never experience the depth of brutality, betrayal, and pain that many heroes of the faith endured. When we think of Paul the apostle or Silas, we love to remember the prison doors opening, the jailer and his family being saved, the songs in the night, the earthquake, and all the people that were saved in their ministry. But the precursor to the victories were stripes laid on their backs, false accusations, public beatings, humiliation, and night after night laying on a cold, hard stone slab with their feet in stocks in prison.

Paul talks about the severe treatment he received at the hands of others in 2 Corinthians 11:23–27, where he says, "Are they ministers of Christ?—I speak as a fool—I am more: in labors more abundant, in stripes above measure, in prisons more frequently, in deaths often. From the Jews five times I received forty stripes minus one. Three times I was beaten with rods; once I was stoned; three times I was shipwrecked; a night and a day I have been in the deep; in journeys often, in perils of waters, in perils of robbers, in perils of my own countrymen, in perils of the Gentiles, in perils in the city, in perils in the wilderness, in perils in the sea, in perils among false brethren; in weariness and toil, in sleeplessness often, in hunger and thirst, in fastings often, in cold and nakedness..."

Considering all the injustice and brutality that Paul experienced, one would think he would become hard and bitter. However, the apostle knew that even in his sufferings God was working out a greater glory in and through him. In Philippians 3:8–10 Paul says, "Yet indeed I also count all things loss for the excellence of the knowledge of Christ Jesus my Lord, for whom I have suffered the loss of all things, and count them as rubbish, that I may gain Christ and be found in Him, not having my own righteousness, which is from the law, but that which is through faith in Christ, the righteousness which is from God by faith; that I may know Him and the power of His resurrection, and the fellowship of His sufferings, being conformed to His death."

Paul knew that suffering was fellowship with Christ, and he said this fellowship of His sufferings will bring me to a place where I am conformed to His death. How do you and I become conformable to the death of Jesus Christ?

Matthew 20:20–23 says, "Then the mother of Zebedee's sons came to Him with her sons, kneeling down and asking something from Him. And He said to her, 'What do you wish?' She said to Him, 'Grant that these two sons of mine may sit, one on Your right hand and the other on the left, in Your kingdom.' But Jesus answered and said, 'You do not know what you ask. Are you able to drink the cup that I am about to drink, and be baptized with the baptism that I am baptized with?' They said to Him, 'We are able.' So He said to them, 'You will indeed drink My cup, and be baptized with the baptism that I am baptized with; but to sit on My right hand and on My left is not Mine to give, but it is for those for whom it is prepared by My Father.'"

Oh, how quickly we boast and answer God, all the while not having any clue what we are asking God to do. These two brothers wanted to enjoy the glory of God's kingdom—they wanted to sit with Him in power and authority and rule and reign with Him over the earth. Can you imagine how the other disciples felt when they heard these two ask Jesus for something as grandiose as this? Scripture tells us that many of them were indignant at their request. Yet Jesus did not mock or ridicule them, but as the Lord always did, He got right to the heart of the question. He said, "You don't know what you are asking for (and they clearly didn't). You want to sit where I am about to sit, but are you able to drink the cup that I have to drink to get to that place where I am going to sit? Are you willing to be baptized with the same Holy Spirit that I'm baptized with? Are you willing to walk in the will of God and to let God's plan and purposes for your life be completely fulfilled, even if it means pain, sorrow, rejection, misunderstanding, scorning, and in some cases even death—are you willing and able to do these things?"

Sadly they answered ignorantly and with much pride, saying, "Oh, we are able."

Christ is really saying to them, "Do you have the ability to drink of wrath which you do not personally deserve?"

Ouch. Of course they were not able to do what the Son of God was indeed going to have to do—die an innocent death on the cross, taking the wrath of God for the sins of mankind onto His shoulders so that you and I could be free from sin and reconciled back to God and to one another.

They had no clue what kind of suffering Jesus was going to endure. Jesus was betrayed by His friend—one of His own disciples, a man in his inner circle. He was betrayed by countless hundreds, and maybe even thousands, whom He had fed on mountaintops, whose children He had been kind to, and healed every kind of ailment and disease—including casting out demons. He had seen this crowd standing before Him and saying, "Crucify Him, crucify Him," and then asking Pilate to release the murderer Barabbas instead of Jesus, the Son of God, the One that had loved them and helped them in every way imaginable.

Jesus knew the hurt of betrayal.

The Lord was treated as a criminal. He endured mocking by the Roman authorities and soldiers. He was abused and battered, suffering such brutality that His face was marred and unrecognizable. The hair of His beard was plucked out by hand. He was punched, whipped, lashed, slapped, and beaten with a stick. The soldiers spit on Him and humiliated Him through their taunting words and their "crown of thorns" that they smashed onto His head.

Jesus knew the pain of abuse—physical and emotional.

The Lord was arrested under false testimony from others and charged with a crime that He did not commit. He did not receive a fair trial. And though innocent, He was given the death penalty.

Jesus knew the hurt of injustice.

Knowing all that He would suffer, Jesus turned to James and John and said, "Are you able to drink of this cup? You want to sit with Me where I am; are you then able to endure rejection? Are you able to endure betrayal? Are you able to endure brutality and abuse? Are you able to face injustice? Are you able to do all these things without losing heart and without losing your focus on God?"

In other words, Jesus is asking them if they can die to self, pick up their cross, and follow Him, no matter where that leads. They want to rule and reign, but are they willing to serve and to be of no reputation before men? James and John answered yes, but not to the suffering and dying to self that Jesus represented. When they answered Jesus that they were able, in their minds they were able to handle the good life, the power, the position, and the honor before men.

Jesus did not promise them the seats next to Him. But He did promise them that they would indeed partake in the suffering that the Son of Man was going to experience. James and John are in heaven—and they are partaking now in the glory of God. But they had to walk in the footsteps of Christ through Gethsemane before enjoying the power of the Spirit working through them.

In Matthew 20:25 Jesus identified the spirit behind this whole interaction with James and John. "But Jesus called them unto him, and said, Ye know that the princes of the Gentiles exercise dominion over them, and they that are great exercise authority upon them. But it shall not be so among you: but whosoever will be great among you, let him be your minister; and whosoever will be chief among you, let him be your servant: Even as the Son of man came not to be ministered unto, but to minister, and to give his life a ransom for many."

Jesus is telling them—and you and me—"If you want to exercise authority, if you want the baptism of the Holy Spirit, if you want to be close to Me so that you can have influence and power, you don't understand the reason that I came to earth. If these are the things you are seeking, you don't understand the heart of God."

God sent His Son to be a servant, to show people the heart of God. And He sent Jesus to be the propitiation for our sins—to be the perfect sacrificial lamb, the only One that could satisfy God's requirement of perfection and complete righteousness.

Jesus is telling us that He came to manifest the heart of God. He came to be God's provision for the need of redemption for a fallen creation. And in order to do so, He became a servant, not a lord, as the Gentiles seek to be. Jesus didn't come to be an earthly king; He came to give His life as a ransom for many.

Are you suffering today? Have you been betrayed? Have you faced injustice? Are you bearing the pain of abuse and brutality?

When we are betrayed, it is a trial like no other. I have experienced the hurt of betrayal. It is a pain sometimes like no other, and some of you were betrayed long before you became a Christian. Your little feet hit the floor, and before you got to be five, you were betrayed. Your pathway became less sure; your steps became feeble. The act of betrayal or abuse became a very, very difficult place for you—like a large hole that swallowed you up, and to this day you still have not been able to climb out. You were betrayed by people whom you trusted.

You were betrayed by people in authority. You were betrayed by people who should have loved and protected you.

So how do you get out of that hole? How do you get past the pain and get to a healthy place where you are walking in the love, peace, and joy of Christ?

The answer is found in one word: forgiveness.

When Jesus was dying on the cross, He prayed to His heavenly Father. Guess what? He didn't pray that God would seek revenge on His persecutors. He didn't call down fire and brimstone to kill those who had betrayed and abused Him. He did something that would forever change the world and show the heart of God: Jesus asked God to forgive those who hurt and betrayed and would kill Him—to not charge them with this offense but rather forgive them. And then with that still, small voice—filled with love and grace—Jesus said, "They know not what they do" (Luke 23:34, KJV).

———◆———

"I was a very hard man," I began to confess in a voice that was soft but rang out clearly. "What I used to do, the employment I used to have, dealt a lot with hurting and dying people. In my heart I became very cold to human need. When I came to Jesus Christ, He changed my heart because I went to Him and said, 'I can't love like You love. I can't care like You care. I don't have the resources in myself. God, You have to do something inside of me. You have to save me.'

"I can tell you tonight that God has been faithful to me because I can stand here and say with an honest heart before you and before God that I love you. I

love you because the love of God is in my heart. God has done a miracle in me, and He has shown me what true riches are in His kingdom. True riches are not material resources or a gathering of spiritual wealth for me, but a taking of what God has given me and sharing it with those around me. This is the kingdom of heaven. This is the church of Jesus Christ. This is the one true gospel of Jesus Christ.

"If anyone tells you anything different," I raised my Bible in the air, *"they haven't spent time in this book, and they have not spent time in the presence of God. Tonight, if you ask Him, He will pour into your heart everything you need. As I have been preaching to you, He has healed my voice. My voice is stronger than when I began. He has touched me. And just as He has touched me, He will touch you!*

"The more we give out, the more God gives to us. He has done a miracle in me just to show you that He can also do miracles in your lives. If you will open your heart and pour out to others, He will heal you. He will strengthen you. He will give you a word from heaven. He will give you everything you need to meet the needs of people all around you. There is nothing more that God needs to do tonight. You have both heard it and seen it.

"Now the choice is yours. Do you want to be a vessel of God's light? Do you want to reach out to your Muslim neighbors? Do you want to reach out to the wounded in your society? Jesus came to His enemies and loved them. The Bible says we weren't even looking for Him when He came to us. But He so loved us that He came to restore us, to heal us, and to give

us power that we might have a gospel to take to our neighbors.

"Church in Jos, you have heard from the Spirit of God tonight. You have seen your enemies subdued. You have watched the devil fight hard to take you and rob you of the treasure of Christ. You have seen the devil fight in the air. You've watched him fight on the ground. And you have seen him defeated."

The crowd applauded. "Nothing can stop you. There is no storm that can stop you. No power of evil can stop you. You are the church of Jesus Christ." The crowd began to shout and wave their hands in the air.

The basis for letting go of our hurts—for not seeking revenge or harboring hate and bitterness in our hearts toward our enemies—is rooted in the act of forgiveness. As Christians, we cannot withhold forgiveness from the one who hurt and betrayed us because God has not withheld His forgiveness of our sins.

THE PARABLE OF THE UNFORGIVING SERVANT

Then Peter came to Him and said, "Lord, how often shall my brother sin against me, and I forgive him? Up to seven times?"

Jesus said to him, "I do not say to you, up to seven times, but up to seventy times seven. Therefore the kingdom of heaven is like a certain king who wanted to settle accounts with his servants. And when he had begun to settle accounts, one was brought to him who owed him ten thousand talents. But as he was not able to pay, his master commanded that he be sold, with his wife and children and all that he had, and that payment be made. The servant therefore fell down before him, saying, 'Master, have patience with me, and I will pay you all.' Then the master of that servant was moved with compassion, released him, and forgave him the debt.

"But that servant went out and found one of his fellow servants who owed him a hundred denarii; and he laid hands on him and took him by the throat, saying, 'Pay me what you owe!' So his fellow servant fell down at his feet and begged him, saying, 'Have patience with me, and I will pay you all.' And he would not, but went and threw him into prison till he should pay the debt. So when his fellow servants saw what had been done, they were very grieved, and came and told their master all that had been done. Then his master, after he had called him, said to him, 'You wicked servant! I forgave you all that debt because you begged me. Should you not also have had compassion on your fellow servant, just as I had pity on you?' And his master was angry, and delivered him to the torturers until he should pay all that was due to him.

"So My heavenly Father also will do to you if each of you, from his heart, does not forgive his brother his trespasses."

MATTHEW 18:21–35

As this parable clearly shows, we have been forgiven the huge debt of our sin by God, so we cannot then turn around and refuse to forgive someone who sins against us. Jesus paid for our sin by dying on the cross. He sacrificed His own life—as an innocent man—to suffer for the sinful actions we have committed. If we truly understand this, we cannot refuse to forgive one another.

A spirit of unforgiveness left unchecked turns into bitterness, which turns into hatred and revenge. And this hardening of the heart is behind some of the worst human atrocities that we have seen in life—including genocide and war.

———✦———

While back in New York, when natural thinking would have suggested that we call off the whole idea of an international outreach in Nigeria, I had remained resolved that we should go. When I arrived in Nigeria, that resolve evaporated. Our advance team was encountering tremendous confusion, corruption, and in some cases outright resistance.

The spiritual warfare had me on my knees wondering if I had made a huge mistake with the international outreach. The admonishment of one of my church elders got me to my feet, and the Holy Spirit gave me the strength and guidance to preach and pray before half a million people. The elder is a brilliant man, a former official of the United Nations, and a Nigerian by birth. When he saw me on the floor, he didn't suggest we pray for strength or guidance. He didn't suggest I take a nap to regain my strength. He scolded me.

"Get up," he commanded gruffly. "You came here to do a job. Now get up and do it."

God apparently knew what I needed more than I did at that moment, and He spoke through our Nigerian-born elder. There was no misunderstanding. He was clear. God was clear. I got up.

Perhaps one of the most potent ideas that God put in my head to deliver to those people was the Jericho

Road story where Jesus declared all religion that has no compassion for its neighbors to be bankrupt. I said it of Christianity and Islam. Both were represented in the crowd. Both had been fighting with each other. Jesus said on the road to Jericho (and I believe He meant for me to echo His words) that religion without compassion is worthless.

Because Jesus is revered as a prophet by believers in Islam, they were not offended by my remark. I anticipated that if anyone might or would be offended, it might be the Christians. But thankfully neither Christians nor Islamists seemed troubled by what I had said. So when they were presented the opportunity to receive Jesus Christ as their Lord and Savior and to walk in true Christianity, which would be demonstrated in how they treated their neighbors, it meant those who raised their hands that night had made a more powerful decision than others who hadn't spent years hating, fighting with, and even killing their neighbors in civil war.

In Nigeria before our arrival Muslims would attack a village and burn churches and the homes of believers. But the believers would retaliate and burn mosques and homes and shops belonging to Muslims. Who can claim a higher divinity in such an economy of violence? I can't speak for the Muslims, but the Christians in the Nigerian civil war were at war against their own God. Once we helped them see that, it made no sense for them to fight anymore but to forgive.

An unforgiving heart can cause a distortion in how we view others and interpret their actions. It's like looking out of a dirty window thinking it's a dark and dismal day when in reality the sun is shining and the flowers are blooming. The power of forgiveness is like wiping the window clean; your whole perspective on life changes instantly. Unfortunately it is one thing to be betrayed by another human being, but sadly there are many who look at their difficult circumstances and feel God has betrayed them. They believe that God wasn't there at their moment of crises or He let them down by not fully meeting their desperate needs. So they live with an accusing heart toward God and because of it blame Him and His people for letting them down.

It is only by recognizing the enormous amount God has *forgiven and wiped the window clean of* that they will ever be able to silence the voice of the accuser.

THE EXAMPLE OF JOSEPH

It's important to look at the life of Joseph to show you that there is a process involved when it comes to forgiving others— especially those who have betrayed and hurt you. It's not just as easy as snapping your fingers and praying some nice little prayer. You have to determine in your heart that you are going to obey and trust God to work in and through your betrayal and pain to bring about His desired will for you. God will comfort you, but He will also shape you into His image. So with His comfort often comes confrontation to school you in the fact that you need His power to love and forgive others— especially those who present themselves as your enemies!

Joseph was subjected to a great amount of betrayal, injustice, and rejection in his life. And as difficult as his experiences were, Joseph stayed close to the Lord and allowed God to mature him and mold him over a long process that would end up saving the lives of the nation of Israel.

Psalm 105:16–22 says, "Moreover He called for a famine in the land; He destroyed all the provision of bread. He sent a man before them—Joseph—who was sold as a slave. They hurt his feet with fetters, he was laid in irons. Until the time that his word came to pass, the word of the LORD tested him. The king sent and released him, the ruler of the people let him go free. He made him lord of his house, and ruler of all his possessions, to bind his princes at his pleasure, and teach his elders wisdom."

Joseph was a man through whom God gave great provision to others in a time of famine. He was the second in command in Egypt and had been entrusted with preparing the storehouses so that people would not starve. Not only did God use Joseph to save the people of Egypt, but He used him to save the nation of Israel through the very family members that had betrayed him as a young man.

You see, before Joseph had great position and authority in the land, he was called to walk a very difficult path.

Some who are reading this are currently walking a very difficult path in life.

They question God: "Lord, I thought this Christian walk of faith was a walk of blessing, provision, and joy. Yet I seem to be called to walk in such a difficult place. I am enduring hardship, while others around me seem to have an easier journey than the one I've had to undertake."

There are some journeys in life that you and I would rather not take. There are some places we would rather not go. And there are some places we would rather not have been. Maybe, just like Joseph, when you were a child, your feet hit the ground with such wonderful expectations of life. I remember as a little boy, I would run out the back door of our house and go into the yard, and I would look up into the sky. I had such a sense that there was something great that was going to happen in my life in the future. I had dreams about what I would be and what I would do. I would look forward to getting up in the morning, running out the door, and living in the anticipation of what was going to happen today.

In the Book of Genesis, chapter 37, we are told that Joseph had a dream. He dreamed that God loved him and that one day he would be in a greatly favored position that God had reserved for him.

As believers, we are all given that dream!

When we come to Christ and are born again, the Lord says, "I have something that only you can do for My kingdom." It may not be grand in the sight of man, but God says it's grand in His sight. He is looking down upon you with favor and will empower you to fulfill the purpose that He has assigned to your life.

Joseph's life became difficult simply when he obeyed his father's request to go check on his brothers. It's then that his brothers, who had long been jealous of Joseph and irritated by his boasting, decided to seek revenge.

We find the story of Joseph's betrayal in Genesis 37:17–33 (NIV):

> So Joseph went after his brothers and found them near Dothan. But they saw him in the distance, and before he reached them, they plotted to kill him.
>
> "Here comes that dreamer!" they said to each other. "Come now, let's kill him and throw him into one of these cisterns and say that a ferocious animal devoured him. Then we'll see what comes of his dreams."
>
> When Reuben heard this, he tried to rescue him from

their hands. "Let's not take his life," he said. "Don't shed any blood. Throw him into this cistern here in the wilderness, but don't lay a hand on him." Reuben said this to rescue him from them and take him back to his father.

So when Joseph came to his brothers, they stripped him of his robe—the ornate robe he was wearing—and they took him and threw him into the cistern. The cistern was empty; there was no water in it.

As they sat down to eat their meal, they looked up and saw a caravan of Ishmaelites coming from Gilead. Their camels were loaded with spices, balm and myrrh, and they were on their way to take them down to Egypt.

Judah said to his brothers, "What will we gain if we kill our brother and cover up his blood? Come, let's sell him to the Ishmaelites and not lay our hands on him; after all, he is our brother, our own flesh and blood." His brothers agreed.

So when the Midianite merchants came by, his brothers pulled Joseph up out of the cistern and sold him for twenty shekels of silver to the Ishmaelites, who took him to Egypt.

When Reuben returned to the cistern and saw that Joseph was not there, he tore his clothes. He went back to his brothers and said, "The boy isn't there! Where can I turn now?"

Then they got Joseph's robe, slaughtered a goat and dipped the robe in the blood. They took the ornate robe back to their father and said, "We found this. Examine it to see whether it is your son's robe."

He recognized it and said, "It is my son's robe! Some ferocious animal has devoured him. Joseph has surely been torn to pieces."

Joseph endured things that would stop most people today in their tracks. They would become crusty and hard and critical. The tenderness of God would be driven from their hearts. I've seen this happen over the years with believers over very small matters—people who have been in the church for years, and they get offended because someone didn't thank them for serving in the nursery, and like a cancer their bitterness grows until they are just taking up space in the pew; there is no engagement with the Lord or fellowship with His people.

Joseph was betrayed by his family—his own flesh and blood. I don't know if there is a deeper betrayal than the betrayal that comes from those that you love, and whom you thought loved you.

For Joseph, the betrayal of his brothers was only the beginning—he would go on to endure other betrayals as well. When his brothers sold him into slavery, he ended up working in the house of Potiphar, an Egyptian ruler. Joseph served Potiphar faithfully. He was a good worker and had exemplary morals and character. But Potiphar's wife was attracted to Joseph and went after him. Joseph continually refused her advances, even literally running away from her as she clutched his shirt. Once again, Joseph faced betrayal when Potiphar's wife accused him of trying to rape her. I'm convinced that Potiphar knew Joseph was innocent, but he chose instead to believe the evil report about him and had him thrown into jail. Yet again, Joseph experienced betrayal even though he had done nothing wrong.

Once again, Joseph refused to wallow in self-pity, so while in prison he worked hard, showing great character and sound moral judgment, and was given a measure of leadership while incarcerated. Having a good relationship with both the inmates and the guards in prison, Joseph's cellmate promised to help him be set free from prison once he was back in a position to do so. But once the inmate got out of jail and went back to work, he forgot all about Joseph. So even in jail, Joseph experienced yet another betrayal.

I don't know about you, but after thirteen years of this I

might be inclined to pack it in, find a cabin somewhere, and just give up.

Are you willing to drink the cup? Are you and I willing to go through the difficult places that we have to go through to get to the place where the power of God can flow through us to those in our homes, our communities, and our cultures?

Thirteen years of living in a difficult place…

The devil's goal was to use these things to hem Joseph in behind the gate of betrayal. The devil would say, "Now Joseph, for the rest of your life, just endure people. Forget about serving people—look where it has gotten you. Listen, it's time you look out for number one—it's time to live your life for yourself. Do what you want, and make the most out of life. After all, staying on the straight and narrow is what got you into all this trouble. Forget other people, and live it up!"

But God had a plan for Joseph—a good plan—and He was using these difficult thirteen years to shape Joseph into a godly leader, one who would save many, many people.

The enemy's plan was to keep Joseph behind the gate of betrayal for the rest of his life. God's plan was to set him free and bring him into his divine purpose.

Though Joseph suffered a great deal, he didn't lose sight of his dream because he continued to walk with God on his path of difficulty. Joseph had an open heart. He allowed God to prune him and mold him into His image.

There are many, many people in the body of Christ who never even come close to fulfilling what God has for their lives. They will get to heaven, but they sit behind the gate of betrayal, saying, "I'll never trust again, I'll never be vulnerable again, and I'll never reach out to people again."

When you stay behind the gate of betrayal, it prohibits you

from having a right relationship with God and right relationships with people. It's exactly the place that the devil wants to keep you in so that you are ineffective in the kingdom of God.

Are you living behind the gate of betrayal right now?

Listen to me, every person who has ever been used in any considerable measure in the kingdom of God has had to go through betrayal. Jesus Christ was betrayed, John the Baptist was betrayed, Isaiah was betrayed, Jeremiah was betrayed, Moses was betrayed, Joseph was betrayed, and the list goes on and on.

You will never amount to what God wants you to be if you can't get through these gates of betrayal. Throughout Scripture we witness men and women who did not stop at the gate but went *through* the gate of betrayal. They went through to the other side—and so can you!

Joseph finally got out of prison, and the Lord opened the door for him to work with the ruler of Egypt. Once again, Joseph worked hard and proved his reliability and was promoted to the second in command in the Egyptian rule. Now he was in the right spot to be the provision needed in the midst of famine—not only for the nation but for those in his family who had wounded him.

When Joseph's brothers first came to him for help, they did not recognize him, but Joseph sure did recognize them. Imagine the thoughts that went through Joseph's mind at that point, not to mention his feelings. Scripture tells us that Joseph spoke roughly to them.

Sometimes that's just where you and I are as well. We can't speak civilly about people who have hurt us. We try to cover it with some Christian words, but there is a roughness in our speech. In fact, there is little of Christ in our words. But rather than defeat, it's the beginning of something that God is doing in us—just as He was doing in Joseph's life.

Joseph's brothers were standing before him, and they were pretending to be honest men. Amazing! They had wounded him, they had betrayed him, and Joseph said to them, "Who are you?" And they replied, "We are all the sons of one man. Your servants are honest men, not spies" (Gen. 42:11, NIV). They were standing before the man they had betrayed, declaring their honesty and integrity!

The most galling thing you will ever have to go through as a Christian is when somebody has betrayed you, and he is absolutely unwilling to admit his fault. He stands before you and exudes an attitude of righteousness.

Joseph is the man who had their provision; he could let them starve to death, and he knew it. He knew there was no hope for them because God had told him there would be a famine in the land that would last seven years. It was within Joseph's power to either help them or not help them.

Though Joseph could have really sought revenge on his brothers, he felt restraint because he feared the Lord. Joseph did test his brothers by putting them in jail for three days, but Genesis 42:18 says, "Then Joseph said to them the third day, 'Do this and live, for I fear God.'"

The fear of the Lord, the scripture says, is the beginning of wisdom. The fear of the Lord moves Joseph to begin to give mercy and provision.

Joseph overhears his brothers talking in their distress. "'We are truly guilty concerning our brother, for we saw the anguish of his soul when he pleaded with us, and we would not hear; therefore this distress has come upon us.' And Reuben answered them, saying, 'Did I not speak to you, saying, "Do not sin against the boy"; and you would not listen? Therefore behold, his blood is now required of us'" (Gen. 42:21–22).

It's incredible that there is no true sorrow in them for what they did to Joseph. Their sorrow is based on the trouble they are facing—the famine—and they feel as if they are basically receiving bad karma for what they had done years ago to Joseph. In the same way, it's like when we get upset about the consequences of our sin but don't feel heartbroken over the sin itself!

Joseph's response to their quiet conversation was to turn around and weep.

God kept working on Joseph's behalf, getting him to slowly unlock the gate of betrayal. In Genesis 43:30–31 we see a yearning for reconciliation growing in the heart of Joseph. It says, "Now his heart yearned for his brother; so Joseph made haste and sought somewhere to weep. And he went into his chamber and wept there. Then he washed his face and came out; and he restrained himself, and said, "Serve the bread."

There is evidence that you are moving to be released from the gates of betrayal when you are yearning now to be reconciled with people who have hurt you. The yearning is birthed in your heart by the Holy Spirit. Even though you've got every reason why you shouldn't forgive them, write those letters or make those phone calls because you are crying out to Christ; there is this yearning that comes into your heart to be reconciled. God puts it there. This is the work of the Holy Spirit within you.

You see, the breaking of the gate is found in forgiveness.

Joseph's heart yearned for reconciliation. His pain was turned to compassion. He had the love of God in his heart, and it flowed out to his brothers. Genesis 45:1–2 (KJV) says, "Then Joseph could not refrain himself before all them that stood by him; and he cried, Cause every man to go out from me. And there stood no man with him, while Joseph made himself known unto his brethren. And he wept aloud: and the Egyptians and the house of Pharaoh heard."

The Lord was flooding Joseph's heart with His love and power to enable him to let go of the hurt and betrayal and replace it with forgiveness and reconciliation.

Genesis 45:3–5 shows us the glorious moment of healing: "Then Joseph said to his brothers, 'I am Joseph; does my father still live?' But his brothers could not answer him, for they were dismayed in his presence. And Joseph said to his brothers, 'Please come near to me.' So they came near. Then he said: 'I am Joseph your brother, whom you sold into Egypt. But now, do not therefore be grieved or angry with yourselves because you sold me here; for God sent me before you to preserve life.'"

The dream that God gave Joseph came true, but he first had to go through a maturing process. That process included humbling and growing Joseph's faith—so much so that when it came time for Joseph's dream to take place, he had the right perspective. It was no longer about him having authority over his brothers (something that he did taunt his brothers about) but about fulfilling God's good purpose and rescuing them! Did you get that? The very thing that Joseph taunted his brothers over when he was young (that his brothers would submit to his authority) became the very thing God used to save Joseph's family and the nation of Israel.

You see, no longer was Joseph interested in having his brothers bow to him—instead, Joseph was interested in saving them. Joseph's difficult thirteen-year journey produced a close walk with God that enabled him to love and care for the very people that had hurt him.

The evidence that you have passed through the gates of

betrayal is when you come to understand that God has been in control of everything all along. Joseph understood the fact that though his brothers meant evil against him, God allowed it because He had a greater divine purpose. This is so important for us to understand. If God allows hurt, suffering, and difficulty in our lives, it's because He has a good plan to use it for a higher purpose—a purpose that He wants to work out through your life.

Romans 8:28 says, "And we know that all things work together for good to those who love God, to those who are the called according to His purpose."

God works *all* things out to conform to His purpose for your life. That means all the things you like and all the things you don't. That means all the things that cause you pleasure and fulfillment, and all the things that cause you pain.

It's time to pray for forgiveness to exude from your life.

You are called to follow in the footsteps of your Savior. You are called to walk with Him. You are called to drink the cup that He drank and be baptized with the baptism of God's love and power. Remember, God loved you in your rebellion; God loved you when you cursed His name; God loved you in your betrayal of Him. It's time to walk through your gate of betrayal and forgive those who have hurt you.

Are you willing to drink the cup?

Mark 9:18 says, "And wherever it seizes him, it throws him down; he foams at the mouth, gnashes his teeth, and becomes rigid. So I spoke to Your disciples, that they should cast it out, but they could not."

When I read the words of the distraught father in that verse, it reveals an accusation leveled at the disciples. What is interesting is the emphasis of the Greek with the words *could not*. It means to have no power, no authority, no strength, or no ability. This was not a casual statement the father made concerning Jesus' disciples. It was an indictment of their lack of spiritual power.

It is evident that the father's feeling of betrayal resulted in his own lack of faith and unbelief toward God. After all, he was a Jewish man who believed he was a child of God. Therefore, why would a loving God allow his son, who was just a child, to be possessed by a demonic spirit? The boy had done nothing deserving of being held captive by Satan. Where was God in his time of need? The father felt betrayed not only by God but also by the disciples.

It's easy to reject or turn away from those who have betrayed you in life. Yet Christ gives us the supreme example when from the cross He prays, "Father, forgive them; for they know not what they do" (Luke 23:34, KJV).

God works through those He chooses and in ways that we would never expect. When news of our upcoming evangelistic rally in the Philippines was announced, a local Pilipino television personality decided to leverage the event to advance his career. Little did he know that God had plans for him.

The Pilipino equivalent of syndicated American TV host Conan O'Brien began to broadcast commentary about our upcoming international outreach and made fun of it. He even went so far as to travel all the way to New York and attend Times Square Church. In a staunchly Catholic nation like the Philippines, the thought of Protestants—Pentecostals, no less—conducting services in the historic Araneta Coliseum in Manila was a temptation he couldn't resist.

Although I never met him when he attended services here, God was at work. The Pilipino television personality gave his life to Christ at Times Square Church and returned to the Philippines a believer. He began to evangelize and promised the Pilipino people they would have an experience like no other when we arrived for the evangelistic rally. The Pilipino people were understandably shocked, amazed, and curious at this man's conversion and transformation.

God didn't stop there. The local organizers, without realizing it, made a major appeal to local Catholics by advertising that our rally would include the Times Square Church Mass Choir. The organizers, of course, meant we were bringing a large contingent of our regular choir, which is quite large. The Catholic locals thought they meant it was a Catholic choir that was going to perform some sort of mass.

The Catholics came out in numbers that only the Pope himself could draw and were very shocked at what they saw and heard. Our choir, which is very gospel oriented, invited people to sing along, clap along, and even dance along. The Catholics were silent and stoic no matter how animated our musicians were.

Natural reasoning would suggest that once word got out following the first night of a three-night outreach, the coliseum would be empty by the third night. But by the third night the coliseum was almost filled for the first time since it was built in 1960. And the

Catholics wound up clapping, singing, and dancing along to our music. Thousands came to Christ that week. The God who can make the impossible possible and united hearts in one accord did it in Manila before my eyes.

———✦———

IMPORTANT TAKEAWAYS FROM THIS CHAPTER

KEY THOUGHT: In life you are not guaranteed that betrayal, even from those close to you, will not happen.

KEY WORD: Forgiveness

KEY INSIGHT: The act of forgiving allows the life of Christ to be evidenced in you.

Chapter Seven
PRAYING FOR FAITH

G EORGE MÜLLER HAD a tremendous heart for God, which also gave him a tremendous heart for people. Besides being an evangelist, Müller was the director of the Ashley Down orphanage in Bristol, England, in the 1800s. He cared for more than 10,000 orphans during his lifetime, established 117 schools that offered Christian education to more than 120,000 children, and traveled (with his wife) more than 200,000 miles (an incredible achievement for pre-aviation times) as an evangelist, sharing the gospel throughout the world.

When asked how he could accomplish so much with so little resources, he replied, "Faith does not operate in the realm of the possible. There is no glory for God in that which is humanly possible. Faith begins where man's power ends."

We could feel the tension the moment we arrived in Burundi. My family and I were put in a compound surrounded by armed guards day and night. The president had assigned guards to me and my family who were part of his elite presidential guard unit because the danger was so real and present. No one knew if our evangelical rallies would reignite the genocide and bloodshed. If that was the sentiment, then I would surely become a target for at least one side of the conflict, as would the president. We both might be targets for both sides. The situation, though quiet, was still volatile.

Burundi was an eerie place. I noticed soon after our arrival that there were no dogs as we had seen running freely in other African nations, such as Nigeria. I asked why there were no dogs and was told that they had all been shot because they became uncontrollable, eating the human bodies in the streets. That helped to remind me how fresh the emotional wounds were. There had scarcely been time for the wounds to close up, much less for scars to form.

I woke up in the middle of the first night in the heavily guarded compound to the sound of screaming and a huge explosion. The guards told me that there was no explosion. They assured me that there was no screaming. It seems I was the only one who heard it. But it was not a dream. I distinctly heard those sounds. I had never heard such sounds before.

A sense of dread came over me that there would soon be another uprising, and I felt guilty that I had perhaps brought our people from New York into harm's way. I got up and went to the rooftop of the guarded compound and paced back and forth for much of the night, reminding myself over and over again what God *had sent me to do. I reminded myself how important it was to simply believe that He was going to accomplish what He promised to accomplish. It required faith, and I was on the spot like never before. "Carter, do you trust Me?" I felt the Lord saying to me.*

———

Our society is obsessed with instant gratification. We don't want to wait for anything. Americans find themselves in debt because they need to have the latest iPhone, television, car, or house by getting loans and credit cards to pay for them. No one wants to save the money to buy that special product—so companies make it possible to gain credit so you can have that product now. College kids get their degrees and want a top-paying job at the top of the executive chain rather than working their way up over time in a company. No matter where we look or what we do, instant gratification is the god of the age. And because of this, we find a generation that is immature, rebellious, and feeling entitled to just about everything—without working hard to gain what they need or want.

But that's not the way the kingdom of God works. Instant gratification is not in God's dictionary because it does not produce faith and trust in Him. In fact, it doesn't produce anything of spiritual worth, nor does it produce godly character.

As believers, we have a tendency to expect instant gratification from the Lord. We pray a handful of times and are distraught if our prayer has not been answered. We might be walking a difficult path in our lives and get frustrated when the Lord does not smooth it out quickly.

His ways are not our ways, the prophet Isaiah said. *His*

thoughts are not our thoughts. He will answer our prayer, but it's in His perfect timing and in His perfect way. He will smooth out our paths but not until He is able to build in us the faith, trust, and character that is needed. Instant gratification does nothing to build one's character or faith. And ultimately God is most interested in maturing us in our walk so that our trust in Him is solid.

Waiting is not easy. But God tells us to be persistent in our prayers, believing that He will indeed answer at just the right time.

Maybe you are tired of waiting for an answer. You've prayed for a specific situation, person, or circumstance, but you have not seen an answer, and you are beginning to lose heart.

Luke 18:1–8 says:

> Then He spoke a parable to them, that men always ought to pray and not lose heart, saying: "There was in a certain city a judge who did not fear God nor regard man. Now there was a widow in that city; and she came to him, saying, 'Get justice for me from my adversary.' And he would not for a while; but afterward he said within himself, 'Though I do not fear God nor regard man, yet because this widow troubles me I will avenge her, lest by her continual coming she weary me.'"
>
> Then the Lord said, "Hear what the unjust judge said. And shall God not avenge His own elect who cry out day and night to Him, though He bears long with them? I tell you that He will avenge them speedily. Nevertheless, when the Son of Man comes, will He really find faith on the earth?"

In this parable there was a widow who continually came to a judge looking for justice from those who had come against her. Though the judge was not a godly man, we can infer from this illustration that Jesus gave the judge the power to make a difference. So this dear widow came to him and said, "Help me—my adversaries are after me."

The judge had the power to help the widow, but the answer didn't seem to be coming. In fact, the longer she appeared before him, the situation most likely was getting worse.

After much persistence by the widow, the judge finally said, "Because of her continual coming to me, lest she weary me, I'm going to get up now and answer her."

At the end of this parable (which means story or illustration), Jesus says, "Shall God not avenge His own elect?"

In other words, if an ungodly human judge can grant the request of a persistent widow, how much more will God answer you (and fight for you) if you call out to Him? God will answer you if you pray in faith.

But God answers on His timetable and in His way, not ours! Verse 8 says, "He will avenge them speedily." God's decision to answer and to help us when we pray will be made quickly. He doesn't ignore our pleas; His character is love, so in all ways He does what is in our best interest.

However, you might not see the answer with your natural eye for a season, even though the answer has come; even though God has decreed that your prayer will be answered, you may not see it. There are reasons for that. Jesus finishes this story about the widow, saying, "But will there still be faith on the earth?"

God is asking us this very question in our instant gratification society: Will there still be the kind of faith on the earth that believes it has the answer and doesn't give up until it is fully seen?

When Christ returns to the earth, will there be a shortage of people who believe and persist in that belief?

Have you been praying for that difficult situation in your life? Have you been praying for your daughter or son who has rebelled and found herself or himself on the wrong path?

God has answered your prayer, but you need to keep praying and believing God that you will see His answer at the right time and in the right way.

The Lord is going to open your prison doors. He's going to give sight to your blinded eyes. He's going to heal your wounded heart. He's going to touch your family and bring them to Himself. He's going to make a difference in your neighborhood. Pray and believe God; trust Him and grow your faith.

Let's take a look at a Scripture passage that really brings the importance of what I am saying to light. Exodus 2:23–25 says, "Now it happened in the process of time that the king of Egypt died. Then the children of Israel groaned because of the bondage, and they cried out; and their cry came up to God because of the bondage. So God heard their groaning, and God remembered His covenant with Abraham, with Isaac, and with Jacob. And God looked upon the children of Israel, and God acknowledged them."

The children of Israel were in a horrible spot. They were being mistreated, facing injustice, and in bondage to the Egyptian government. These people cried out from the depth of their hearts: "God help us; don't You see what's happening to us? We are Your people. We're being corralled like cattle; we're being oppressed, ridiculed, mocked, controlled; we're not free the way You said we should be free."

Have you cried out that way to the Lord?

The people of Israel knew the promise that God gave to Abraham—that they would be a blessed people and nation and that they would be a blessing to all those who are upon the earth. I imagine they were wondering what happened to the blessing!

So as a people, they cried out to God collectively. They cried out because of the oppression. They cried out because the society all around them was marginalizing them and using them for their own good and vilifying them as believers in the living God.

God heard their cry instantly, and He acknowledged them. In other words, it technically means that He accepted them as His own people and He answered their cry.

Exodus 3:7–10 says, "And the LORD said: 'I have surely seen the oppression of My people who are in Egypt, and have heard their cry because of their taskmasters, for I know their sorrows. So I have come down to deliver them out of the hand of the Egyptians, and to bring them up from that land to a good and large land, to a land flowing with milk and honey, to the place of the Canaanites and the Hittites and the Amorites and the Perizzites and the Hivites and the Jebusites. Now therefore, behold, the cry of the children of Israel has come to Me, and I have also seen the oppression with which the Egyptians oppress them. Come now [this is to Moses now He's speaking], therefore, and I will send you to Pharaoh that you may bring My people, the children of Israel, out of Egypt."

Now I want you to take a journey with me in your mind. God heard the cry, and He looked down, and He said, "I'm going to answer you. I'm going to deliver you—your answer has come."

Now the people of Israel are crying out to God constantly. God could have snapped His fingers and opened the borders. He could have created an army out of nothing. He could have sent angels to rescue His people. Or He could have just caused all of Egypt to die right on the spot.

He could have answered in so many ways, but instead, He chose a way that more than likely wouldn't have been Israel's first choice. In fact, if it was you and me praying through this situation, it would not be the way we would want God to do things! Instead of an instant miracle answer, God goes into the desert and finds an old man who's eighty years old and calls him to rescue His people! While the Lord is doing all of this, Israel is still crying out for help.

The point is, God has heard the cry of His people—He has not ignored it. Even though the people have not seen the answer yet, God is already working out His answer to rescue them. He's called a man named Moses to be His representative to Pharaoh in order to let His people go—but first He has to deal with Moses and his problem of unbelief.

Once Moses gets through his training camp with the Lord, he has to go to his father-in-law and ask for permission to leave. Once he has done that, he's got to convince his brother, Aaron, that he needs to go with him. Finally he needs to pack everything up and go to Egypt.

Even while on his journey to Egypt, Scripture tells us that Moses was not fully engaged yet with the work that God called him to do. He was still somewhat apprehensive and not fully believing and relying on God, and he almost died because of it.

We don't know exactly how long it took from that first cry of Israel to their rescue, but we know that from the time God says, "I've heard you, and I've answered you," to Moses going to Pharaoh it took quite a bit of time. Nevertheless, it doesn't change the fact that God answered the prayer and put His plan of rescue into action the moment He heard His people's cry!

There is an important lesson for us in this story. Due to our inclinations for instant gratification—instant answers—we often think our prayers are falling on deaf ears. Instead of being persistent in prayer and having faith, we throw our arms up and say, "What's the use!" We need to understand that, as God's children, He *does* instantly hear our prayers. Our cries to God do not go ignored—they don't fall on deaf ears. He is fully aware of our situation and our heart's cry. And just as importantly He is not failing to answer our prayers. In fact, God answers all of our prayers, but we need to understand that He does so in His way and in His perfect timing. Sometimes His answer is yes, no, or wait.

God wants you and me to keep praying with a heart of faith. He will not withhold any good thing from His children, but He will do what is in our best interest, and sometimes that is not what we think is best. Time and again, the Lord has shown me that His plans for my life are far better than anything I would orchestrate. This is where faith comes in. We need to have faith that God will do what is best for us—whatever that may be.

When you cry out to God, please take heart and *know* that the Lord has heard your cry!

Moses finally shows up in the camp of Israel and tells them the story of God appearing to him in a burning bush. He tells them that God has called him to stand before Pharaoh as His representative and to tell the Egyptian leader he needs to let God's people go.

Exodus 4:31 says, "So the people believed; and when they heard that the LORD had visited the children of Israel and that He had looked on their affliction, then they bowed their heads and worshiped."

Praise God—they believed!

———◆———

The first public speaking I did in Burundi was to a national pastors' gathering in advance of the evangelical rally. Several thousand Hutu and Tutsi pastors were there.

"If you are going to propagate the division in this country," I told them, "there will be no power in your religion. It will be pointless. There will be no healing or restoration. You will be the ambassadors of deeper division, and tragically it will be in the name of God. As spiritual leaders," I went on, "you have the obligation to model the cross of Jesus Christ and teach forgiveness, even for those who have killed your loved ones and would kill you."

At that meeting, with the pastors from across Burundi and Rwanda, I gave an altar call for those who were willing to forgive. I knew that if God did not break down the division in the clergy, forgiveness among the people would be hopeless. But this was His intention all along. I was only His vessel.

There was a stunned silence among the several thousand Tutsi and Hutu pastors in attendance when I opened the altar. Finally, in the silence several pastors came forward. Nobody was praying. Nobody was speaking. Then suddenly one of the pastors kneeling before the altar began to wail. His wail that pierced the heavy silence was like nothing I had ever heard before.

All I could think of was that this must be the sound of a person coming home to find his or her family *murdered. It wasn't a cry. It was a haunting wail that sent chills up my spine. And then one man's wail became two and continued to spread like a fire throughout the crowd. It was the wailing of men whose families had been murdered.*

I knelt down at the edge of the platform and hugged two men, and we sobbed together. Their tears mingled with mine on my cheeks and on theirs. This went on for nearly twenty minutes.

Wailing broke down into heaving sobs that seemed to have been stored under pressure for years. Then, from the depths of the sobbing, an incredible joy broke out.

The wailing that had given way to sobbing gave way to dancing and shouting and hugging. It was astonishing to watch, even for those of us who had not witnessed any of the tragedy leading up to this moment. It was a Joseph moment. Joseph had to cry before he could forgive and embrace his brothers who had left him for dead. It was that breakthrough, that victory that followed us onto the field night one of the three-night evangelical rally.

I can't emphasize enough how important it was that the pastors of that region experienced the power of the Holy Spirit and the victory of faith. If they had not experienced what they did, it wouldn't have mattered what I preached to the crowds. The pastors would have undermined it. Our work there would have been wasted. God knew that and broke down the barriers between them that would have been impossible to dismantle in the natural.

I always find that the Lord is creative in His answers to prayer. Only God could use an eighty-year-old man with a stick in his hand and his eighty-three-year-old brother with a one-line sermon to rescue the entire nation of Israel!

Thank God that His ways are not our ways and His thoughts are not our thoughts!

But Even After They Believed, Things Got Worse

After hearing the good news that the Lord had heard their prayer and would deliver them, even though it did take some time, they expected the good news to follow. But each time Moses went to Pharaoh to direct him to let God's people go, things only became worse for the people of Israel. As Pharaoh continued to harden his heart toward God, the Jews were the bearers of his wrath.

Exodus 5:21–23 says, "And they said to them, 'Let the Lord look on you [this is now to Moses and Aaron; the children of Israel are speaking in verse twenty-one] and judge, because you have made us abhorrent in the sight of Pharaoh and in the sight of his servants, to put a sword in their hand to kill us.' So Moses returned to the Lord and said, 'Lord, why have You brought trouble on this people? Why is it You have sent me? For since I came to Pharaoh to speak in Your name, he has done evil to this people; neither have You delivered Your people at all.'"

Instead of things getting better, the situation was getting far worse. The people were experiencing more hardship and brutality at the hands of Pharaoh. And because of this, their faith was turning into hopelessness.

It's my personal opinion that God needed to make sure that everybody wanted to get out of Egypt. If you remember, there were people who were divided on the issue of leaving. Though many were crying out for freedom, some enjoyed the rich foods and the pagan cultural influence. They may not have liked the enslavement, but they liked the other aspects of Egyptian life.

God wanted to rescue His people for good. He didn't want them having one foot in Israel and one foot in Egypt. He didn't want them looking back. So the heat was turned up so that Israel understood just how deplorable their situation was and would want to leave it behind.

When I think about this, I think about how the Lord works in our lives to get us to be completely loyal to Him. God does not want you or me living with one foot in the Spirit and one foot in the world. A divided heart never brings about the will of God. So even in our own lives sometimes the Lord has to turn up the heat in the situation we are in so that we realize it is time to stop trying to live with one foot in the flesh and the other foot in the Spirit. It doesn't work.

The Lord often needs to bring us to a place where we realize just how vile the flesh really is so that we will give ourselves wholeheartedly to God and to His kingdom. Remember, the Lord's will is that we would grow in faith and bear fruit for His kingdom and for His glory.

The people's faith is beginning to fail, and even Moses cries out to God and says, "Why did You send me here? You gave me a promise, but Your promise is not being manifested."

That's why Jesus says, when He comes back, "Will He really find faith in the earth?" Will there be anybody left that believes that God is exactly who He says He is and that He is faithful to the end?

Mark 9:22 says, "And often he has thrown him both into the fire and into the water to destroy him. But if You can do anything, have compassion on us and help us."

But if *You* can do anything…

This was the question posed to Jesus by the father of a son who was demon possessed. Jesus replied and said, "If thou canst believe, all things are possible to him that believeth" (Mark 9:23, KJV).

In essence, Jesus was saying, "Life under the dominion of Satan's kingdom doesn't have to continue." The kingdom of God overcomes the kingdom of Satan just as light overcomes darkness. You only have to flick the light switch on once to become a believer that light is more powerful than the darkness. The issue wasn't if God could perform the impossible but rather, could the father *believe* He could?

Friend, the issue is the same today! God has already won the victory for you. He paid the price for your sin on the cross, and He rose—conquering the power of death and darkness in your life. The issue isn't whether God can; the issue is whether you believe He can. The Old Testament was based on a *do* relationship with God: "Do this, and you will be delivered." The New Testament is based on a *faith* relationship with God: "*Believe* this, and you will be saved."

Maybe you have been praying for years for certain family members, and you are believing in faith that God is answering your prayer. In fact, you may see signs that the answer is coming. Then all of a sudden, it seems like everything is against you. Every thought that hell could produce is bombarding your mind. Now you find yourself in a place of doubting, and you are thinking, "What is the use? Where is God? I thought I saw a glimmer of hope that an answer was coming, but now everything is a mess."

Doubt tosses us back and forth like a ship on a rough sea.

"Did I really hear from God? Did God really give me that kind of a word?"

It's in the midst of the storm that Jesus turns to you and says, "Do you trust Me? Do you have faith in Me?"

The distraught father recognized that neither he nor the disciples had power in themselves to bring about the deliverance of his son. But here was a man called Jesus standing before him saying, "If you believe, *all things* are possible with God." This was a crucial moment for the father—he was being confronted with his own lack of faith in a God who had created the universe by a single command. The realization impacted him so powerfully he began to weep. With tears streaming down his face—of course he believed all things were possible with God—he realized he needed help in believing God would set things right for him and his son.

With a single command Jesus delivered the boy from the stronghold of Satan. The light went on, and darkness departed in an instant. Such is the power of God through faith!

Faith in Christ is the foundation for everyone who comes to God; no one is exempt from God's divinely designed plan.

—◆—

I had been praying privately for God's favor in my teaching as well as fervently praying with our staff and worship team that God would be glorified in everything we did. The night I spent pacing the rooftop, I also prayed God's covering for our international

*outreach team. Pacing and praying on the rooftop,
I recall saying aloud, "God, I know why You sent
me here, and I know that You will accomplish this
through Your power. I will simply do what You called
me to do." And that prayer required me to have faith
that God would see His will done in a setting that
was more explosive and dangerous than anything I
had ever faced in my life.*

The Example of Elijah

When Jesus asked the father of the demon-possessed son how
long he had been that way, the man replied, "Of a child"
(Mark 9:21, kjv). In other words, it had been a long time.
It was this long, ongoing difficulty that sparked the father's
desire to seek God's help. God will use the difficult seasons in
our lives to bring about a desire to seek Him and to have faith
in His deliverance.

Take, for example, Elijah. James 5:17 says, "Elijah was a
man with a nature like ours, and he prayed earnestly that it
would not rain; and it did not rain on the land for three years
and six months." Elijah knew that his prayer would bring
about unprecedented hardships upon the nation. This was necessary because the king of Israel had led the people down a
sinful path. In essence, Elijah wanted the nation to turn back
to God and was prepared to pray to that end, even if it meant
it would take three and a half years to be answered. Basically
Elijah was saying, "Whatever it takes, Lord, whatever it takes!
If it takes hardships to break them away from the grip of a
sinful direction, do it."

Now God could say immediately after Elijah prayed that is was done—it was answered. But there's a season between when the prayer is prayed and the answer is manifested. You can pray for family members who are not believers, and God can say, "Done! I've heard your prayer, and the answer is on the way...but it's going to take some time. I need to allow them to go through difficulties so their desire is turned from the world to Me." God can say to you, "Your son is going to come home. Your daughter's going to come home." The moment you believe God, He calls it faith.

When you read about the whole event in 1 Kings 18, Elijah's prayer was answered immediately when he prayed it, but God had a special timing for Elijah to see his prayer completely fulfilled. It takes time, so don't give up! For three and a half years all false comfort would have to be taken away from Israel. The people had become satisfied living without God—their cupboards were full, and their stomachs were satisfied. They needed to go through hard times to realize that they needed God.

As long as everything looked good and they had plenty to eat, they didn't need God, but once the Lord dried up their crops and emptied the bread from their cupboards, they would discover life without God was difficult. All those false prophets who had been telling them the evidence of Baal was in their prosperity were now seen for who they really were, "false prophets."

When Elijah prayed a second time after the three and a half years of drought, the floodgates of heaven opened and gave the land rain. The earth produced its fruit, and the people knew it was from God because their hearts had been turned back toward the Lord.

Again in 1 Kings 18, the Bible tells us that Elijah had prayed seven times. He never gave up because he didn't see the evidence on the first prayer. Remember, we started with the parable about the widow who kept coming to the judge; over and over again, she just kept going until she obtained the answer she needed.

Jesus asked, "When the Son of Man returns, will He find this kind of faith on the earth, this kind of faith that says, 'O God, send the rain of heaven. O God, give us an awakening one more time. O God, send your Holy Spirit. God Almighty, let Your glory fill the earth.'"

When the disciples came to Jesus and asked, "Why could we not drive the demon out?" Jesus said to them that this kind of demonic possession only comes out with persistent prayer and fasting. In other words, "Don't give up if you don't see the answer immediately." But God has promised to do this, and God will do it.

Hallelujah to the Lamb of God—glory to the name of Jesus!

———◆———

If we do not love other people, the Bible says we are not yet perfected in God. The Bible says if any man says, "I love God," yet hates his brother, he is a liar. I took that message to a nation where the wounds of genocide were still open and seeping. As I mentioned, I didn't go to Burundi to win a victory; I went there to declare God's victory. The president God gave Burundi in those days was a man who was seeking God's heart. Through President Nkurunziza, God began the healing.

In my closing message to the crowds in Burundi, I explained how, two thousand years ago, after Jesus was crucified and after He rose from the dead, 120 people gathered in a room. They were living in the middle of a society that was looking for vengeance. Everywhere they walked, people were talking about violence and vengeance. But they had begun following the One who had told them they must forgive to know His power. Christ's truth about forgiveness truly spanned the centuries as I spoke to the Burundi people.

I told the Burundi crowd that the world was going to see them walking in unity, and people from other nations, especially those from neighboring countries, were going to say they have never seen this before. I predicted that those who witnessed them walking in unity would ask, "Where do they get the power to do this, to forgive like this?" I predicted that Rwandans who had seen their own awakening aborted would say, "We see men and women of different tribes in Burundi embracing and loving each other. Where do they get the power to do this?"

If we are willing to open our hearts and let Jesus Christ come in, if we receive Him as our Savior, if we are willing to agree with God to turn us from old things to His truth, we must also ask God to fill our hearts. And we need to simply believe God—to have faith!

I publicly thanked President Pierre Nkurunziza and his wife for their graciousness toward Teresa, to me, and to our volunteers and musicians from Times Square Church in New York. President Nkurunziza's visit to our worship service in New York had led to the Burundi rallies, and his love for the Lord and desire for a lasting peace and unity among his countrymen was unwavering.

The Bible says when the righteous are in authority, the people rejoice. There was rejoicing during our time in Burundi and for a decade afterward. President Pierre Nkurunziza was righteous authority and was the beginning of God's blessings on that nation.

⎯◦⟐◦⎯

WHAT KIND OF FAITH DO YOU HAVE?

But when the Son of Man comes, will He find that you have this kind of faith on the earth?

Do you have the kind of faith that believes God for situations that are impossible in the natural, that kind of faith that says, "I will not let go of my sons and my daughters. I will not let go of my marriage. I will not let go of my faith—even though my situation looks hopeless, I trust God will hear my cry?

"God, I cry out to You, for You are the only One who can make a difference. I cry out to You, God, for issues in my own character that I can't change. Your Word says a leopard can't change its spots. I can't change this about my character. But O God, I cry out to You, Lord, to send the answer into my heart. Send the answer into my life, and supernaturally give me victory in this area of my life.

"O God, I've carried this wound around in my life far too long. I walked the streets, Lord, mourning like a dove, day in and day out. O God, You're the only One who can heal my heart because You promised that You would come and heal those that have been bruised in heart.

"So I cry out to You, God, and I ask You, Lord, for the healing that You've promised. You say that out of weakness we are made strong. You say in Your Word that You take the foolish things of this world to confound the wise. O God, help me now to do something that will glorify Your name. Fill me with Your Holy Spirit, O God; give me the strength that can only come from You, and make a difference through my life.

"I lift up the people that I know, the people in my community, the people in my office, the people I see on the street every day who seem so indifferent to truth. But You know their heart, and there's something arising in this generation. There's a cry now coming into it. I can hear it now. There's a cry in this generation!"

There are so many people who cry themselves to sleep at night. They don't know God; they have no way out; they feel nothing but hopelessness.

We need to press in and pray; casual prayer will not meet the need of this hour.

When the Son of Man comes, will He find faith on the earth?

Will He find faith in *you*?

Will the Lord find Christians who are not spiritually lazy, who are not looking for instant results but somehow understand the character of God that when we call out to Him, He will answer. We might not see the answer with our eyes, but we know He will answer, and we know we will live to see the day when God answers our cry.

Psalm 126:6 says, "He who continually goes forth weeping, bearing seed for sowing, shall doubtless come again with rejoicing, bringing his sheaves with him."

———◆———

By the end of our third night in Burundi, the joy of the Lord broke out so powerfully that the entire crowd was dancing. They danced so wildly that they stirred up a large cloud of dust that covered the entire area. President Nkurunziza was dancing, his vice president was dancing, and the government officials and their wives were dancing. Those in the first fifty rows or so on the field who had plastic chairs held the chairs above their heads as they danced. I picked up my plastic chair on the platform and held it above my head as I danced with them.

That was the night we knew the victory was complete. In a place that had known violence such as few on earth have ever experienced, the government officials, especially President Pierre Nkurunziza, would have had no idea whose gun the assassin's bullet would have come from if there had been one. If a coup was being planned, our evangelical rallies would have made a coup very convenient for the conspirators. The prior two presidents had been assassinated by their own military.

But God had other plans. God built a hedge of protection around President Nkurunziza. God built a hedge of protection around all of us. The awakening that happened in Burundi, the sudden awareness of God that causes such wild celebration, is happening now more and more often in our Tuesday evening Worldwide Prayer meetings at Times Square Church, where our worshippers in the theater are joined via internet by fellow worshippers in nearly two hundred countries and terri-tories who text and email their prayer requests.

There have been times when the Spirit of God has come upon us so powerfully that all we can do is cry out. When the Lord begins to do His mighty work among His people who are humbled before Him, the outcry is deafening. What is deafening to us is the sweetest sound God can hear—the prayers and praises of His people.

IMPORTANT TAKEAWAYS FROM THIS CHAPTER

KEY THOUGHT: Answers to prayer may take time.
     Don't give up!

KEY WORD: Persistence

KEY INSIGHT: Difficult times may follow after you pray.
     Believe God knows what He is doing in using
     hard times for His own glory and purpose.

Chapter Eight

PRAYING FOR PEACE

A ND THE PEACE of God, which passeth all understanding, shall keep your hearts and minds through Christ Jesus" (Phil. 4:7, KJV).

It is not only possible to have peace in the midst of darkness; it's a promise that Jesus gives to all who believe on Him.

Are you in a dark place today? Are you praying for God's peace to fill your heart and mind?

You may be thinking, "Yeah, but you don't know the trials I am facing right now." And you would be right, I don't. But God does. And His promise of peace in the midst of your circumstance is exactly what He can and will give to you.

Consider the following true story.

In 1873 a successful businessman lost all his material possessions in the great Chicago fire. This did not trouble him too much, for he had set his affection on "things above." However, just a few weeks later, when his wife and children were on board the *Ville du Havre* en route to France, their ship was rammed by an English vessel and sank within two hours, claiming the lives of 226 people. Although his wife survived, all four of their children perished in the icy waters.

The man was given the tragic news and later shown the spot in the mid-Atlantic where the shipwreck occurred. Although heartsick with grief, Mr. Spafford suddenly felt an inrush of supernatural peace and comfort as he looked to the Lord for strength. With tears streaming down his face, he picked up a pen to record his feelings, and from his well-blest heart flowed these thrilling words:

> When peace like a river attendeth my way,
> when sorrows like sea billows roll;
> whatever my lot, Thou hast taught me to say,
> "It is well, it is well with my soul."[1]

When God told Times Square Church to preach in Jamaica, our advance team, led by Loretta Busch, searched for the best space in which to hold an evangelistic rally. There were many suggestions of scenic locations around Kingston. But a pastor from an impoverished small church spoke up and said, "You should hold the rally where the problem is. And that's Trench Town."

The pastors and local organizers gasped at the idea of going into this demilitarized zone controlled by drug lords. Tens of thousands of people lived in that ghetto with extremely high unemployment rates. The Jamaican government had sent the military into Trench Town to clean it up in 2001, and the drug lords defeated the military, driving them from the area. Many died in those bloody battles.[2]

But in the midst of the tumult and the danger of the area, the peace of God filled our hearts, so that's exactly where

Times Square Church chose to erect a platform and hold four nights of evangelistic rallies.

—◆◆◆—

No one likes to get bad news.

You can be going right along with your daily activities, and then in an instant everything in your life can change—a phone call, a report, a vehicle accident, a pink slip, or something else that rocks your world can take place. It doesn't even have to be a calamitous event to change your life in a moment of time.

Have you experienced that? You are cruising right along in life, but then your husband comes home from work and says he wants a divorce, and your world comes crashing down. Or you wake up as usual to get ready to go to work, but once there, you find out you no longer have a job, and like that, your world falls apart.

Maybe you are saying, "Pastor, you are speaking right to me. I remember the moment when the doctor told me I had cancer, and everything I had leaned on, everything I had trusted in, all that I had built, all that I thought was going to give me security—all of it came crashing down around me."

Can we have peace in our hearts when our world is turned upside down?

Jesus said, "Peace I leave with you; My peace I give you. I do not give to you as the world gives. Do not let your hearts be troubled and do not be afraid" (John 14:27).

The kind of peace that the world gives is conditional—it stands on a shaky foundation that can change with every passing whim. Some people find peace and security in money, until they lose their job or the stock market crashes. Other people find peace in relationships or in their marriage, until they fail. The kind of peace that Jesus promises His children is unconditional. It's a peace based on the foundation of God Himself—unchanging, loving, gracious, merciful, and faithful. God's peace is not dependent on our circumstances; in fact, it thrives in the midst of our trials, tribulations, and dark valleys.

The peace that Jesus gives you and me is drawn from the very heart of God. It's a peace that reminds us in the deepest of our trials that He is faithful, He keeps His promises; it assures us that we are His and that nothing—no person, no demon, no fear, no enemy—can take us out of God's hand; and it comforts us with the truth that we are secure in Him.

The peace of God in your life gives you the sense that you are not walking alone; God is walking with you. God's peace tells you that you do not have to sustain yourself; God is sustaining you. The peace that Jesus gives assures you that you don't have to get through the storm because God's voice is calming the storm and making a way through impassable waters.

When our lives change—when we find ourselves in the midst of difficult storms—we witness the power of God like we have never seen before. When the children of Israel stood at the banks of an incredible and impassable sea with an army bent on destroying them in hot pursuit, they witnessed the power of God to do the impossible.

THOUGHTS OF PEACE, NOT EVIL

Jeremiah 29:4–11 (KJV) says:

> Thus saith the LORD of hosts, the God of Israel, unto all that are carried away captives, whom I have caused to be carried away from Jerusalem unto Babylon; Build ye

houses, and dwell in them; and plant gardens, and eat the fruit of them; Take ye wives, and beget sons and daughters; and take wives for your sons, and give your daughters to husbands, that they may bear sons and daughters; that ye may be increased there, and not diminished. And seek the peace of the city whither I have caused you to be carried away captives, and pray unto the LORD for it: for in the peace thereof shall ye have peace. For thus saith the LORD of hosts, the God of Israel; Let not your prophets and your diviners, that be in the midst of you, deceive you, neither hearken to your dreams which ye cause to be dreamed. For they prophesy falsely unto you in my name: I have not sent them, saith the LORD. For thus saith the LORD, that after seventy years be accomplished at Babylon I will visit you, and perform my good word toward you, in causing you to return to this place. For I know the thoughts that I think toward you, saith the LORD, thoughts of peace, and not of evil, to give you an expected end.

Notice what God says in the first verse written here: "Thus saith the LORD of hosts, the God of Israel, unto all that are carried away captives, whom I have caused to be carried away from Jerusalem unto Babylon..."

Do you see it? God is talking to His people about their captivity (displacement), and He says "whom I have caused to be carried away." In plain language nothing comes our way that God hasn't allowed for a specific reason. When you are a child of God, nothing, and I do mean nothing, can touch you without going through God first!

No matter what fiery trial, troubling situation, or displacement that you face, you are not in the hands of the devil—you never will be. You are in the hands of God. He says to you, "Listen, I have allowed this to happen for your eventual good."

There can be many reasons that the Lord has allowed you to go through the difficulty that you are facing right now. He can be getting your attention, drawing you away from a particular sin, seeking your growth, causing things to fall in place in order to bless you and others, and the list can go on. No matter what dark valley we walk through, God uses it to teach us to trust Him.

Instead of striving to get out of our situation, or murmuring about our misery, God wants us to lean on Him and trust Him. When we recognize that God is in control—even in the middle of our darkness—and that His plan is good and for our benefit, we can get up each day and live unto Him and rest our heads on our pillows at night in perfect peace.

God's people were living in Babylon—a wicked and idolatrous society. Yet the Lord tells His people, "Build ye houses, and dwell in them; and plant gardens, and eat the fruit of them; Take ye wives, and beget sons and daughters; and take wives for your sons, and give your daughters to husbands, that they may bear sons and daughters."

In other words, He told His children to keep on living—"Work, have a family, and walk with Me *in* your difficult circumstances." The bottom line is this: bloom where you are planted.

No matter what your situation is or where you end up, the word of the Lord is: "Where I have allowed you to go, bloom there. Dig down deep where you are, and see what I am going to do in and through you!"

Remember Joseph, whom we talked about in the previous chapter? Joseph didn't want to be sold into slavery. He didn't want to be in prison. But instead of living in misery and anxiety, Joseph had the peace of God and bloomed where he was planted. In each difficult place Joseph found himself, he dug in deep, trusted the Lord, and excelled in everything he did. In the end Joseph understood that what his brothers meant for evil God meant for good.

This is so important to understand. No matter how horrible our circumstances are, we can enjoy the peace of God. How? By trusting God's character—that He is good. In the last part of the scripture in Jeremiah, the Lord tells us that His thoughts toward us are of peace, not of evil, to bring us to an expected end. When we believe in our hearts God is good— that His thoughts toward us are peaceful and that He is going to bring us through to the other side—we are able to rest and enjoy God's peace no matter how strong the storm around us!

In the Book of Jeremiah, God goes on to say to His people, "And seek the peace of the city whither I have caused you to be carried away captives, and pray unto the LORD for it: for in the peace thereof shall ye have peace" (29:7, KJV).

Wherever you are, whatever you are facing, pray! Pray for the place that God is moving you to. Pray for the people who are a part of your difficult circumstances. Whatever you are facing in this season that God has allowed into your life, live as a person of God in it! Live in such a way that God is honored and receives glory. The nonbeliever will watch a Christian closely as he goes through a fiery trial. That's where the rubber meets the road. What's this Christian going to do now that he is in a bad place? By "blooming where you are planted," you do more to share your faith by being a living testimony.

God has to have a people in this generation that say, "Though the mountains be shaken out of their place, though the seas overflow their borders, I will not be afraid. I will trust in God. My confidence is in God. God will not fail me; God will not forsake me; God will give me a testimony in the midst of my enemies."

The Lord says in Isaiah 30:15, "For thus saith the Lord GOD, the Holy One of Israel; In returning and rest shall ye be saved; in quietness and in confidence shall be your strength" (KJV).

Notice it doesn't say "in murmuring and anxiety shall be your strength!" Too often that's how we respond when facing a dark valley in our lives. Now, don't get me wrong, I realize how hard our struggles can be. I'm not making light of your problems or mine. *But* in order to have God's peace and strength, it is in how we respond to the trial, more than the trial itself, that we find victory.

"In quietness and in confidence"—in other words, having a calmness in the midst of the storm. The Lord doesn't want you to panic or run amok trying to figure a way out of your situation. Instead, He asks you to stand still—stand still and see the Lord fight this battle for you, stand still and see God provide for you, stand still and see God work out this trial for your good.

David said in Psalm 23:2, "He maketh me to lie down in green pastures: he leadeth me beside the still waters" (KJV).

Listen, as a child of God, you will be led into places by the tender voice of our Savior. No matter what you are facing, God will be with you, and you will be given promises of comfort, reassurance, and peace. Your quiet and calm spirit, combined with your confidence in God, will stand out in stark contrast to the many people screaming into their phones and cursing the Lord in the midst of their struggles.

If Christ is in you, you will make it to the finish line. You will see that the light at the end of the tunnel is not a train but God Himself. You, my friend, will pass through your fiery trial and make it to the other side.

———◆———

On the first night, a small smattering of nervous Christians from the surrounding area gathered in "no-man's land." They sort of huddled together in front of the platform we had erected. There were two police officers who looked more nervous than the church ladies who had been brave enough to come out with their Bibles in their arms. There simply wasn't much of a rally to speak of on the first night; thirty acres with just us and a handful of believers, perhaps several hundred at most, nearly all of them from surrounding towns and villages, not Trench Town. Everyone was half expecting to duck for cover when the shooting started.

The presence of evil was so strong in that place, it was palpable. And we were then as we are now, prayer warriors. Even the local churches had been praying 24/7 for over a month before our arrival—praying that God would cover us and the rally. Still, Satan's grip on that real estate was powerful. The witchcraft and demonic spirits were hard at work against us.

What we didn't know on that first night was that out in the darkness, beyond our sight, "no-man's land" was surrounded by several thousand people who were looking on from their respective neighborhoods, afraid to step into the demilitarized zone for fear of mass bloodshed. No drug gang trusted the other not to fire on them. So the Trench Town dwellers stayed behind an invisible fence and ventured no further.

I sensed that we were in the spiritual battle of our lives. I know I was in one of the most frightening spiritual battles of my life—fear of the flesh against the power of God. I called Times Square Church the following day and spoke to David Wilkerson. I explained our dilemma and asked for his guidance and most of all his prayers. It was Sunday afternoon when we spoke, and Pastor Dave stood up in the evening service, approximately twenty minutes before night two of our evangelistic rally in "no-man's land" was about to begin. He asked the church to pray for us. He led the worshippers at Times Square Church in prayers that Satan's power would be broken.

Look again in the chapter we have been studying about a father who has a son possessed by a demonic spirit. Nothing can be more daunting than seeing your own flesh and blood beleaguered by the enemy, especially when you are powerless to do anything. This was what the people in Jamaica were experiencing in a far greater measure. They felt powerless concerning the drugs and gangs that pervaded their neighborhood. But God comes to bring hope to the hopeless. "And ofttimes it hath cast him into the fire, and into the waters, to destroy him: but if thou canst do any thing, have compassion on us, and *help* us" (Mark 9:22, KJV, emphasis added).

In this verse you see a cry of *hope*. In reality all hope of seeing his son live a normal life had all but evaporated. The only resource left to him was God.

Hope and faith are closely intertwined. You cannot have

true life-changing faith without hope. Yet the full realization of what is hoped for is only obtained by faith.

Using an acrostic, HOPE can be described in four ways that spells out faith:

H—HELP (Mark 9:22): In the Greek it means to bring aid or to relieve the oppressed from the oppressor. The Old Testament is full of amazing stories of how God came to rescue His people. In fact, throughout the Scriptures, God's people were encouraged to come to Him when the enemy was oppressing them, and He would deliver them.

The source of hope is a desire that God will come to the aid of His people.

O—OVERCOME (Mark 9:22): The devil has one agenda, and that is to steal, kil,l and destroy (John 10:10). This child was being thrown into the fire and water in repeated attempts to kill the child. Yet with one command from Jesus we enter into the power and victory of Christ.

The outcome of hope is faith. This faith leads you to an overcoming life.

P—PEACE (Mark 9:24): When you've exhausted all your own resources and have come up empty, the place to go to find perfect peace is with Christ. This father appealed to the only One who could help. It would be here where he would find the peace he needed in the midst of the storm.

The result of hope manifested is an undeniable rest in God's power.

E—EXPECTATION (Mark 9:24): We have already discussed that the greatest cause of discouragement is unmet expectations. If any expectation of freedom for the possessed child was going to be achieved, it would have to be on God's terms. He never disappoints because He is God. He does, however, have an expectation on us. He expects us to *believe* on the One He sent.

The continuing hope is that God will be there for us all the days of our lives.

Unfortunately there is a loss of hope in our world. Even inside the doors of churches, people are living in a place of shattered dreams.

Maybe you can relate. You once had great hope in your heart. You once sang a song that had endless joyful verses in it. But then your world turned upside down. Now you find there's deep sorrow in your heart, and you can hardly sing your song anymore. It seems that despair comes knocking at your door every day, trying to take away the shred of hope that you still hold on to for the future.

Our world is filled with people who have given up! They had hope for the future; they had dreams and aspirations that now seem irretrievably lost. The enemy of our souls is always trying to confirm our feelings that all hope is lost—*but it's not true*! As believers, we are never without hope. Yes, we experience what seems to be setbacks and great loss, but the truth is that even these difficult situations in our lives are all part of God's plan—a plan that brings about His good and peace, not evil.

When we understand that God is working behind the scenes, and we fully put our trust in Him, He will work out *all* things for our good. *Hope* is always a part of our lives because God is the One holding on to us and directing our paths. Time and again, in His way and in His timing, the Lord *always* brings us through the darkness to the sunlight.

Jesus said, "These things I have spoken to you, that in Me you may have peace. In the world you will have tribulation; but be of good cheer, I have overcome the world" (John 16:33).

THE PEACEMAKERS

Matthew 5:9 says, "Blessed are the peacemakers, for they shall be called sons of God."

God gives us peace in the midst of darkness not to keep it to ourselves but to, in turn, go into the world and testify that what God has done for us He can also do for others.

How can we make a difference in our dark world? Is there a way to speak for God that will make people turn toward truth and find the hope and peace that only God can give?

Jesus' ministry on earth gives us examples of what our speech and life should look like.

His earthly ministry was about loving people—He encouraged them, He served them, He healed them, He gave them clear direction and brought them into the right focus, and He brought them back to life. By showing them the character of God, He loved them into the kingdom.

As the Lord's disciples, we are His representatives in the world today. We are His peacemakers, helping people to see the God who loves them and has reconciled them back into fellowship with Him. I believe Jesus left us a picture of what we, as believers, are called to do in the world.

The Weeping Woman

John 20:13–16 says, "Then they said to her, 'Woman, why are you weeping?' She said to them, 'Because they have taken away my Lord, and I do not know where they have laid Him.' Now when she had said this, she turned around and saw Jesus standing there, and did not know that it was Jesus. Jesus said to her, 'Woman, why are you weeping? Whom are you seeking?' She, supposing Him to be the gardener, said to Him, 'Sir, if You have carried Him away, tell me where You have laid Him, and I will take Him away.' Jesus said to her, 'Mary!' She turned and said to Him, 'Rabboni!' (which is to say, Teacher)."

How did Jesus choose to come to this woman in her hopeless situation?

The scripture says Mary turned around, and when she saw Jesus, she assumed He was the gardener! She didn't recognize Him. Jesus could have appeared however He wanted to—He was raised from the dead, all powerful, and with all authority. But He chose to appear to her as an ordinary person.

I believe He was showing us the purpose and pattern of His church—just ordinary people, like you and me, coming to somebody in a hopeless situation.

He appears as a gardener! Don't you love that—the risen Christ appears to Mary in her time of despair as a gardener? We too often look for God in the big, miraculous happenings in life, not understanding that He can be found in the still, small voice; He can be found through the encouragement of normal, ordinary people. When I was a new pastor in Canada, renovating an old church building that we bought, I was in a place of despair—overwhelmed by the enormity of the work and the lack of workers to help me. God came to me in that despair and encouraged me—not through a thunderclap of miracles—but in the quiet, tender words of two little old ladies who walked into my church (not even being members of it) at the right time.

Jesus looked at Mary and said, "Why are you weeping?"

I'm sure that the tone of the Lord's voice was tender—that it rang out with concern and compassion because it opened the floodgates of Mary's distress. She poured out her heart to this "gardener" and pleaded with Him that if He knew where Jesus' body was, to please let her know so that she could attend to Him.

Mary needed compassion. She loved Jesus and was distraught, not only that His body was not in the tomb but that her dreams and her hopes regarding the Messiah had been shattered.

We need to be people who reach out to those who are hurting and discouraged with the compassion of Christ. Our words need to be tender, caring, and authentic. Mary poured her heart out to who she thought was the gardener! She felt safe doing so!

What about you? Are you approachable? Do you give people the assurance that you care—that they are safe to open their hearts to you?

Jesus replied to Mary's despairing questions with one word: "Mary!"

Jesus said her name as only God can say it. He said her name with assurance, He said her name with confidence, and He said her name with the authority of One who had the ability to sustain her!

Isaiah 43:1 says, "But now thus saith the LORD that created thee, O Jacob, and he that formed thee, O Israel, Fear not: for I have redeemed thee, I have called thee by thy name; thou art mine" (KJV).

We serve a personal God. You and I are not just mere blips

on God's radar screen. He is personally acquainted with us because He created us. He knows us and calls us by our name.

There are a lot of people in the world who are crying out in despair who need to know God hears them, knows them, and calls them by their name. The point is that you and I are not called to be superstars; we're not called to have all the answers. We are simply called to be ordinary people with faith and compassion who share the love of God with those who are in need.

There's been more done in my life through ordinary believers with tender words of assurance than any prophet who's ever lived in the kingdom of God. The Lord has accomplished much in my life through people who just said, "It's going to be OK. God is with you. He's going to keep you; He's going to help you."

On the Road to Emmaus

Luke 24:13–27 says:

> Now behold, two of them were traveling that same day to a village called Emmaus, which was seven miles from Jerusalem. And they talked together of all these things which had happened. So it was, while they conversed and reasoned, that Jesus Himself drew near and went with them. But their eyes were restrained, so that they did not know Him. And He said to them, "What kind of conversation is this that you have with one another as you walk and are sad?" Then the one whose name was Cleopas answered and said to Him, "Are You the only stranger in Jerusalem, and have You not known the things which happened there in these days?"
>
> And He said to them, "What things?"
>
> So they said to Him, "The things concerning Jesus of Nazareth, who was a Prophet mighty in deed and word

before God and all the people, and how the chief priests and our rulers delivered Him to be condemned to death, and crucified Him. But we were hoping that it was He who was going to redeem Israel. Indeed, besides all this, today is the third day since these things happened. Yes, and certain women of our company, who arrived at the tomb early, astonished us. When they did not find His body, they came saying that they had also seen a vision of angels who said He was alive. And certain of those who were with us went to the tomb and found it just as the women had said; but Him they did not see."

Then He said to them, "O foolish ones, and slow of heart to believe in all that the prophets have spoken! Ought not the Christ to have suffered these things and to enter into His glory?" And beginning at Moses and all the Prophets, He expounded to them in all the Scriptures the things concerning Himself.

When you read this Scripture passage, the first thing that strikes me is that these men were walking away from Jerusalem and toward Emmaus. Jerusalem is the place of promise; it's the place of God's intended coming kingdom on earth. But these two men were walking away from Jerusalem. They had been there to see Jesus. Like others, they had heard all about Him and were filled with hope that the Messiah had finally come. Yet now they were walking away from the city. Their dreams were shattered; they had lost hope.

Suddenly this stranger came walking along beside them. They didn't know it was Jesus—they didn't recognize Him. Yet the Lord came alongside them and walked with them. I love this! Jesus doesn't abandon us when we are confused and despairing. He doesn't walk away.

Here's the bottom line: We need to be willing to walk beside those who are hurting. We need to invest in people's lives.

Jesus walked with them and listened to them as they shared their disappointment and despair in what happened to Jesus on the cross. It's important to note that Jesus didn't interrupt them when they were pouring out their hearts. He didn't cut them off and blast them for their wrong perception or thinking. The Lord let them get everything off their chest! They're talking to the One who'd just been beaten to death, nailed, and crucified for them, and they had already lost confidence in Him.

After they had shared their heart with Jesus, the scripture says: "And beginning at Moses and all the Prophets, He expounded to them in all the Scriptures the things concerning Himself."

When we are walking alongside people, we need to open the Scriptures up to them and help them understand that suffering, sorrow, confusion, and darkness do not mean that we've lost the battle. We have to be able to explain to them, just as Jesus did to the men walking toward Emmaus, that it was the plan of God to send His Son to earth, to have Him die on a cross for the sins of the world, to be placed in a grave, and to be raised again from the dead on the third day so that forgiveness, life, and victory could be brought back to those who put their confidence in Him.

The reality is that darkness has to come before the dawn. Suffering has to come before victory. I think we have allowed a gospel to be preached in our nation that tells people that if you come to Jesus, it's just going to be sunshine all the way. But that's not the true gospel. God works in and through our suffering to bring about faith, growth, and fruit. We never learn the hard lessons of life in the sunshine; we learn them when our way is cloudy and dark because it is then that we stop leaning on our own understanding and abilities and lean instead on the Lord.

Jesus was gentle with these men—and when they invited Him to stay, He stayed. Though their eyes still were not open to the fact that He was the Lord, they found themselves encouraged by His sharing of the Scriptures, and they wanted to know more!

Jesus was patient and attentive to these men. In the same way, we need to be patient with people who don't have a grasp of the truth of God's Word. People who have embraced a certain view of God don't change that view overnight. We need to be gentle and patient. We need to walk with them and invest in their lives.

God will not abandon you in times of confusion. He will not walk away from you when you have questions that you don't have answers for. He's not a fair-weather friend who takes off when hard times come. Jesus walks with us. He talks with us. And He doesn't leave us!

The Fishermen

> Afterward Jesus appeared again to his disciples, by the Sea of Galilee. It happened this way: Simon Peter, Thomas (also known as Didymus), Nathanael from Cana in Galilee, the sons of Zebedee, and two other disciples were together. "I'm going out to fish," Simon Peter told them, and they said, "We'll go with you." So they went out and got into the boat, but that night they caught nothing.
>
> Early in the morning, Jesus stood on the shore, but the disciples did not realize that it was Jesus.
>
> He called out to them, "Friends, haven't you any fish?"
>
> "No," they answered.
>
> He said, "Throw your net on the right side of the boat and you will find some." When they did, they were unable to haul the net in because of the large number of fish.
>
> Then the disciple whom Jesus loved said to Peter, "It is

the Lord!" As soon as Simon Peter heard him say, "It is the Lord," he wrapped his outer garment around him (for he had taken it off) and jumped into the water. The other disciples followed in the boat, towing the net full of fish, for they were not far from shore, about a hundred yards. When they landed, they saw a fire of burning coals there with fish on it, and some bread.

Jesus said to them, "Bring some of the fish you have just caught." So Simon Peter climbed back into the boat and dragged the net ashore. It was full of large fish, 153, but even with so many the net was not torn. Jesus said to them, "Come and have breakfast." None of the disciples dared ask him, "Who are you?" They knew it was the Lord.

JOHN 21:1–10, NIV

At the initiation of Peter, the disciples went out fishing. After all the things they had been through, they went back to what they knew. But after fishing all night long, they came up empty.

There are some people who give up on their faith when things get hard. Yet if your relationship with Christ is real, you will find that going back to your old life simply doesn't work. You will come up empty time and again. And here are the disciples, going back to their old life but coming up empty.

While all this is going on, Jesus is making breakfast. He could have done what Elijah did with the prophets of Baal and mocked them. He could have criticized them or even ridiculed them. But He didn't. It was not in Jesus' character to do any of that. He chose instead to serve His distraught disciples. He simply made biscuits and fish on a fire. I love this!

Jesus deals with us in the way that our hearts need. He came to Mary with compassion. He walked with the men on the road to Emmaus, showing patience. And here, with His disciples, He comes to them as a servant.

While preparing the meal, Jesus finally asks the disciples, "Have you caught anything?"

The disciples yelled from the boat, "No!" Now you know these men were becoming men of truth because I don't know a single fisherman who tells the truth when you ask him if he's caught anything!

Jesus responds to the disciples by saying, "Throw your net on the right side of the boat and you will find some." Jesus never did anything just for the sake of doing it. There was always a divine purpose to everything He said. And here, in this instance, He was trying to help His disciples get back to their calling—get back to the place of victory.

Cast it on the right hand of God—the place where God's power is. Preach the cross of Jesus Christ! Preach the victory of the resurrected life in Jesus Christ. Preach about turning away from the old and turning toward the new.

When people are hopeless all around you, tell them who Jesus is; tell them what Jesus did. Tell them about the gospel— the victory over sin, hell, and death. Tell them about the kingdom of God and the power of the Holy Spirit. Tell them about the newness of life that God promises to those who will trust in Him.

You see, that's what the church looks like, ordinary people who believe in God, trust Him, and live in His peace in spite of their storms and their dark nights! We don't know all the answers to life's problems, but we know the One who holds the answers.

"To give light to those who sit in darkness and the shadow of death, to guide our feet into the way of peace" (Luke 1:79).

At that moment in the message, I pulled back from the pulpit, and I began to call out to God. I realized that only God Himself could change this moment in history and make it work for His glory. No amount of preaching, praying, or praising in and of itself would release this crowd from the grip of Satan. Suddenly it occurred to me that only God could raise this place— these people—from the dead.

As I began to cry out, "O God, O God, O God," a weeping came on me. I was overcome by weeping, and I sobbed, "O Jesus, help these people. O God, come and give them life." The service came to a halt. The crowd couldn't hear what I was saying as I sobbed. They just heard my wailing and saw my chest heaving.

Though I wasn't aware at that moment, I was told later that the weeping spread through the small crowd and began to infect the crowds on the edges of the field. A woman who was at a booth way in the back looked at a man standing near her; the sawed-off shotgun was plainly visible in his belt. He was a thug by anyone's definition, armed and dangerous, perhaps responsible for one or more of the killings that took place every month on every acre in "no-man's land."

Despite his exposed weapon and outward appearance, he was weeping along with the rest of us. His tear-filled eyes met the woman's eyes. Her instinct was to look away in fear. But the man gestured toward the stage in the distance, and he said to her, "That man is crying for me. Do you see that? He is crying for me."

<hr>

Important Takeaways From This Chapter

KEY THOUGHT: In a troubled world where there is no hope, Jesus still calms the storms that give us fear and anxiety.

KEY WORD: Peace

KEY INSIGHT: God can use anyone, including you, if you have a genuine love for people and a desire to see them delivered out of the grip of Satan.

Chapter Nine

PRAYING FOR FREEDOM

THE EMAILS KEEP increasing in number.

The online prayer site is teeming with requests.

The circumstances may be different, but the desperation in their voices is the same.

From North York, Canada: I have severe depression. I want healing. Pray for me. I can't eat or sleep. Pray for me. Help me.

From New York: Pray for Alicia, for God to deliver her from depressed spirit and low self-esteem. I pray that she will return to the Lord and serve Him. Pray for my father, who needs healing from wasting away, a depressed mood, that help would be provided to care for him.

From Queens: Pray for my son who joined the army and is suffering from deep depression and has turned to drinking and smoking.

From Colorado: I am in a deep, dark fog of depression. I can't get free, and I have no energy to go to church. Please pray for my relationship with Jesus.

From New Westminster, Canada: Pray for my nephew. He is severely depressed. He is only twelve years old. Pray for deliverance, salvation, and a restoration of the family.

From Florida: Urgent. I am a single mother in total despair. Deep soul wounds, depression, years of severe pain. I was in an accident with a young son today. Pray for wholeness.

From Colorado: I am living with my girlfriend and just existing. My parents are divorced, and I don't have a church in Colorado. I am buried in compromise. Please pray for a miracle.

The prayer requests come in from all around the world. And the troubles are immense and seemingly insurmountable:

- Depression

- Anxiety

- Poverty

- Divorce

- Substance abuse

- Rebellious children

- Lonely people

The list can go on and on.

What about you? Are you in a difficult place? Do you feel trapped—imprisoned by your own emotions, circumstances, or behaviors?

You are not alone.

There is good news for you today. Jesus died on the cross to set you free—you just need to recognize your moment of freedom!

The city of Rosario, Argentina, sits at the conver-
gence of highways from Santa Fe to the northeast and
Córdoba to the northwest, linking up on the way to
the capital city of Buenos Aires. When the Lord called
me and the Times Square Church international outreach team to Argentina, our advance team discovered a tribe of forgotten people living in the Rosario
city dump. Our team members were searching for
appropriate sites for an evangelistic rally, and the
local guides kept leading them to nice parks and fields
in the more affluent parts of Rosario. But when members of our team were driving back to the airport, they
got lost and wound up near the dump. There they
found a group of forgotten people who, like the Twa
in Burundi, had no hope of escaping that life.

Generation after generation, they were born in the
dump, grew up in the dump, and died in the dump.
There was no school for the kids, and there were no
jobs for the adults other than waiting for the dump
trucks to arrive and dump their loads. The people
then dug through each pile for anything of any value,
no matter how small or how filthy. They lived with
the poorest sanitation imaginable. There was no fresh
water, just a stream of filthy waste filling the ditch
that ran through the dump.

Previous evangelical outreaches had pandered to
the rich and middle classes of that region. But we
made the dump our project. The evangelical rallies
and the work of the Times Square Church medical
and construction teams ultimately motivated the local
churches and government into serving these poor dump
dwellers. For the first time in their history, the kids

were allowed to go to school and were given clothes and supplies. Fresh water was piped in, replacing the muddied stream that had once been their only source of water.

The government built much-needed housing—another tremendous first for these dear people of the dump. Donations from Times Square Church set in motion giving from many Christians across Argentina, the United States, and other countries, who gave generously and helped to pave roads in these neighborhoods for the first time.

The love of God, demonstrated through the loving hearts and service of His people, won souls to Christ. The Lord did a powerful work through the evangelistic rallies and hard work of medical and construction volunteers.

The prosperity Christian leaders of Argentina wept at what God had opened their eyes to see. They began working with the poorest of the poor for the first time in a meaningful way.

God made these invisible and forgotten people visible in a way that only God can.

John 1:1–3 says, "In the beginning was the Word, and the Word was with God, and the Word was God. He was in the beginning with God. All things were made through Him, and without Him nothing was made that was made."

The above scripture is a phenomenal statement. John is recognizing that the person of Jesus Christ was in the beginning with God when the worlds were created—when darkness turned into light, when boundaries were established, and when humankind was created out of the dust of the earth.

Jesus Christ was there with God—moving with and in unison with the Father. All things were made through Him. In other words, Jesus Christ exercised the full authority and power of God! In Him was life, and this life was the light of man.

The apostle John continues to say, in John 1:14, "And the Word became flesh and dwelt among us, and we beheld His glory, the glory as of the only begotten of the Father, full of grace and truth."

A lot of people know *about* Jesus Christ—including unbelievers. And many Christians can say, "I know that He is God. I know He was in the beginning with God. I know He has the power to create a galaxy with the spoken word of His mouth. I know all these things." But the apostle John goes beyond knowledge when he says, "Then we saw Him. He manifested Himself to us, and we saw Him and His glory, as 'the only begotten of the Father, full of grace and truth.'"

In other words, they experienced God—they knew Him personally. They were impacted by Jesus' willingness to touch their lives in such a profound way that their very lives were changed.

Knowledge is a good thing, but if it doesn't lead to a personal experience with God, we are not entering into the knowledge of the truth. Let me stress a very important fact to you: even the demons acknowledged that Jesus was the Son of God! James 2:19 says, "You believe that there is one God. You do well. Even the demons believe—and tremble!"

When Jesus confronted a demon-possessed man, the demons "fell down before Him, and with a loud voice said, 'What have

I to do with You, Jesus, Son of the Most High God? I beg You, do not torment me!' For He had commanded the unclean spirit to come out of the man. For it had often seized him, and he was kept under guard, bound with chains and shackles; and he broke the bonds and was driven by the demon into the wilderness. Jesus asked him, saying, 'What is your name?' And he said, 'Legion,' because many demons had entered him. And they begged Him that He would not command them to go out into the abyss" (Luke 8:28–31).

Knowledge of God alone is not enough. The demons had knowledge of who Jesus was—they knew He was the Son of God, and they knew He had power over them, but they did not follow Him.

There is a difference between head knowledge and heart knowledge. There are many Christians who have not come to the knowledge of the truth within their hearts. They are still living in bondage to behaviors, sins, habits, and feelings because they have not come to the place of recognizing the reality—the truth—of the Word of God in their lives.

It's one thing to know about the Lord and another thing to see Him—to come to the realization of who He is and what He has done for *you* personally.

There comes a time when the Word manifests and becomes real in your life, in a moment of time like the twinkling of an eye.

Luke 4:15–21 shows a moment of recognition of the reality of the Son of God. The passage says:

> So He came to Nazareth, where He had been brought up. And as His custom was, He went into the synagogue on the Sabbath day, and stood up to read. And He was handed the book of the prophet Isaiah. And when He

had opened the book, He found the place where it was written:

"The Spirit of the LORD is upon Me, because He has anointed Me to preach the gospel to the poor; He has sent Me to heal the brokenhearted, to proclaim liberty to the captives and recovery of sight to the blind, to set at liberty those who are oppressed; to proclaim the acceptable year of the LORD."

Then He closed the book, and gave it back to the attendant and sat down. And the eyes of all who were in the synagogue were fixed on Him. And He began to say to them, "Today this Scripture is fulfilled in your hearing."

Imagine being in the synagogue on that specific day and time and hearing Jesus, the very Word of God in the flesh, read the Old Testament prophecy about the coming of the Messiah and finish the reading by closing the book and saying to everyone seated in front of Him, "Today this Scripture is fulfilled."

The people of Israel had been waiting and looking for the time when the Messiah would come. They had been anticipating the day of their salvation—the day they would be set free. And here Jesus declares their day has come—their freedom is right before their eyes. How did they respond? Did they jump up and down and praise God for their day of visitation? No, they did not recognize their moment! They had memorized this specific scripture—they knew what the Bible taught, but they did not recognize the day of their freedom. The Son of God was standing right before them, and in spite of all their biblical knowledge they did not recognize this moment of truth.

I am reminded of a time that the Lord came to Elijah. He spoke to His dear prophet in the midst of Elijah's depression. God said to him, "What are you doing here?" In other words,

"Elijah, you know who I am! You know I can keep you, you know I have all power, you know I have all authority, and you know I have called you. Elijah, you don't belong here! You don't belong in depression. You don't belong in bondage. You don't belong in despair. Elijah, you have the Spirit of God in and on you now!

Today, as a believer, you are in a place where your knowledge of God and His Word can be experienced. The truth that you see in God's Word and have believed for salvation can jump off the page (and out of your head) and truly come alive in your heart and in your sight. God is speaking to you today just as He spoke to Elijah.

Jesus said that *today* (right before your eyes) this scripture is fulfilled in your hearing! Everything that is mentioned in this passage can be yours. Your heart can be healed. Your prison doors can open. You can understand the treasure of heaven that now belongs to you. Today, His very presence can come alive in your heart!

Daniel had been praying for years for Israel's freedom from captivity. Three times a day he opened his window toward Jerusalem based on the promise and the Word of God. And suddenly, after many years, God's Word popped off the page! Why? Because this Word is *alive*! It is the Living Word of God! It is not just a history account! Daniel said, "O God, You are going to set Your people free! Hasten the moment, Lord; hasten the moment that I have seen in Your Word." Daniel had been reading the Word, but now he saw it!

There is a difference between reading something and seeing it.

Do you understand yet this moment of recognition? Do you know you can be free? Do you know that this is a moment to pray and fight and regain what the enemy has taken away?

I know what it's like to feel poor. I know what it's like to grow up with very little hope. I know what it's like to walk the streets as a teenager intoxicated and angry. I know what it's like to look into the future and see emptiness. I know what it's like to be completely bound by fear. I know what young people feel in our generation. I know how the poor man feels. I too was beaten up by the enemy, and I was deeply wounded in my heart.

In my former angry, sullen, drunken adolescent state I recall often walking past a particular church with white siding in my hometown. I only found out years later that it was a born-again Baptist congregation. They once had outdoor meetings and exciting worship, but the city shut them down and even threw the pastor in jail. The church went to court to fight the prohibition against their outdoor meetings and won. But for some reason, even though they won the legal right to worship outdoors, they refrained from doing it.

That church never knew that there was a depressed and drunk kid walking past its doors on a regular basis, but no one came out to reach him. The kid never knew that there was eternal life and joy inside those doors until he would eventually be converted by a Royal Canadian Mounted Policeman named Irv.

I was that kid. Maybe you were too.

I was left on the road half dead. But somebody came to me and opened his heart. He opened his home and

*began to speak words of life into my heart. He poured
the love of God into me. Because of it I found Jesus
Christ as my Savior. I found the life that God gives
to those who trust in Him. And God by His mercy
has called me into ministry. But I've never forgotten
where I came from, and I've never forgotten what the
gospel is all about.*

*The Scriptures show us that the congregation that
followed Jesus wasn't made up of the most religious or
the wealthiest people. In fact, the religious could not
understand Him. But the poor, the blind, the prosti-
tutes, the lame, the lepers, and those whom society
didn't want—they became Christ's congregation. And
He loved them and poured His life into them. Most
importantly they knew He loved them.*

*Have you experienced the freedom that only Jesus
Christ can give? Has the Lord poured His life into
yours?*

———⊰•⊱———

When someone looks or acts differently from us, we have a
tendency to avoid that person or hold him at arm's length, and
all too often this is repeated again and again in the church. But
Jesus was different; when you read the Gospels, you see how
often He made the disadvantaged the center of His ministry
and the recipients of His healing power. There is an interesting
verse written by the prophet Ezekiel that was inspired by the
Holy Spirit to help him capture the whole essence of the heart
of God. Ezekiel 18:4 says, "Behold, all souls are Mine." In
the context of this incredible statement, Ezekiel was referring

to a son who was set at variance to his father, and vice versa. Ezekiel points out that God wasn't calling out who was in the wrong and who wasn't. Instead, he was showing that God's love is for all souls, whether it is the sinner or not.

Ezekiel's words include you too, beloved. You are at the very center of the love and compassion of God no matter how well you have done or how you have failed Him in the past. This chapter is about *freedom*. It is about how you can be healed and set free through Christ, the Son of God.

In every chapter I have endeavored to highlight a partic-ular portion of Scripture from the Gospel of Mark that fol-lows a father and his disadvantaged son. The boy was being involuntarily held captive by the devil, and Jesus was the only One who could set him free. John 10:10 says, "The thief comes only to steal and kill and destroy; I have come that they may have life, and have it to the full" (NIV). Freedom from such satanic strongholds was at the heart of Christ's ministry, and it must remain the message of the church if it wants to remain relative to a confused world. The father of the pos-sessed boy didn't want to hear a message that gave him ten steps on how to live with a demoniac son; he wanted to see the power of God set his son free once and for all. It reminds me of Moses and how God sent him to Pharaoh, not with a message on how to treat God's people in a kinder, gentler way. No! Moses was sent in the power of God with just one message on his lips: *"God says, 'Let My people go.'"* There weren't going to be any half measures with God. It was to be a total deliverance for every man, woman, and child. Acts 7:35 says, "This Moses whom they refused, saying, Who made thee a ruler and a judge? The same did God send to be a ruler and a deliverer by the hand of the angel which appeared to him in the bush" (KJV). The word *deliverer* in the Greek is *lutrotes,*

219

which means to set at liberty or to set free by the means of a ransom or atonement. God said to Moses to take the message of freedom to the Israelites; God and not the hand of man would deliver them.

Freedom for the demon-possessed boy took on the same message that Moses spoke to the Pharaoh. Freedom came by Christ proclaiming to the kingdom of darkness to loose and set the child free! The Bible says, "When Jesus saw that a crowd was running to the scene, he rebuked the impure spirit. 'You deaf and mute spirit,' he said, 'I command you, come out of him and never enter him again'" (Mark 9:25, NIV). In that moment Satan's power was defeated and the kingdom of God was established.

True freedom results in three clear manifestations:

- The kingdom of darkness is defeated, and its power, nullified.

- The individual can move on in life without the past debilitating controls of Satan.

- The person is restored in his relationship with God and with man.

Jesus stood in the temple and said, "I've come to see prison doors opened. I've come to set the captives free. I've come to heal those who are wounded and hurting. I've come to give sight to the spiritually blind. I've come to preach the Good News of God to the poor. This is why I've come."

And Jesus said to His disciples, "As the Father sent Me, even so now I send you. You are to minister to the poor. You are to set the oppressed free. You are to touch those who are wounded with the healing touch of almighty God."

———

In the Gospel of John, in chapter seven, Jesus was attending the Feast of the Tabernacles. It was an important tradition that celebrated the time when the people of Israel were finally set free from the bondage of Egypt. Remember how God used Moses to free His people? And though they were set free from the captivity they suffered under the Egyptians, they still had yet to enter into their full inheritance of the Promised Land.

The people of Israel were more or less halfway between their former bondage and their future promise. Now that identifies with a lot of people—including Christians!

It was on the last day of the Feast that Jesus stood up and cried out, saying, "If anyone thirsts, let him come to Me and drink. He who believes in Me, as the Scripture has said, out of his heart will flow rivers of living water" (John 7:37–38).

Jesus is crying out today as He was crying out then! Are you tired of just living halfway to victory?

In other words, you aren't living in victory, but you aren't living in bondage either. Being in Christ, you can point to certain former behaviors that you have been set free from, but there are still existing problems that you have not defeated.

Do you feel as if you are dwelling in a booth halfway between your old way of living and what you're supposed to be in Christ? Are you fully aware that you're not living in the victory that God prescribed for you?

The apostle Paul describes it this way in Romans 7:18: "For I know that in me (that is, in my flesh) nothing good dwells; for to will is present with me, but how to perform what is good I do not find."

Paul gives a succinct definition of the human condition. We know what is right; we know what we should be doing, but we can't find the power to do it! In other words, in practical terms, "I know I should forgive those who wounded me, but I can't forgive them." "I know I should be a person of truth, but I find that when my mouth opens, that crookedness in my character still keeps coming to the surface and causes me to say things in a way that I shouldn't say them."

There are so many things that we know we need to do, but we can't find the ability to do them. Paul goes on to say in Romans 7:19–22:

> For the good that I will to do, I do not do; but the evil I will not to do, that I practice. Now if I do what I will not to do, it is no longer I who do it, but sin that dwells in me. I find then a law, that evil is present with me, the one who wills to do good. For I delight in the law of God according to the inward man.

In other words, Paul is saying, "I've got this element of my former bondage. It's still clinging to me; it still wants to control me; it still wants to govern my life. I don't know how to get away from this!"

Can you relate to Paul's words?

I know as a husband, I should love my wife as Christ loves the church. I know as a wife, I should respect my husband. I know as a child, I should obey my parents. I know as an employee, I should be giving my all (as working unto God). I know I should be trusting God for my provision and for my future. I know I should be content in the Lord and not always wringing my hands, wondering if I will ever get married.

So Paul is recognizing what God's Word says, and in his heart he delights in God's righteousness, but he also knows that there is another law inside of him that wars against what he knows is true, and it is this law that wants to bring him back into bondage, back into the captivity of the law of sin, which is in his members.

Paul, like the rest of us, finally cries out and says, "O wretched man that I am! Who will deliver me from this body of death?" (Rom. 7:24). In other words, how will I ever get free and become the man (or woman) that I'm called to be? I have a high calling of God in Christ Jesus, but I'm not living where I'm supposed to live.

I don't speak the way I'm supposed to speak, and my eyes don't see the way God's calling me to see! I feel as if I'm living somewhere between bondage and promise. And quite frankly, I'm tired of this. I'm thirsty, Lord; I'm exhausted trying to be all that God wants me to be.

Dear fellow believer, I know how you feel because I traveled this path years ago. I know exactly what you're feeling. You're doing your best to be holy; you're doing your best to walk right and to speak right and to do right, but almost every day you come home with your head down.

You know you're not going to hell, and you know heaven is going to be your home, but you are tired of living between bondage and promise! In fact, you are thirsty for more of God, but you feel broke. You have no more resources. You have nothing more to spend.

You cry out, "Is there a place of victory for me? I thirst!"

And that's the cry of many people today.

Paul comes to a glorious conclusion and gives us the answer to our human condition. He says, "I thank God—through Jesus Christ our Lord! So then, with the mind I myself serve the law of God, but with the flesh the law of sin" (Rom. 7:25).

The Lord is calling you to Himself. It is by His power that you are given victory—not of yourself. God wants to release His full provision into your heart.

Let's look at the example of King David. Though King David was deeply flawed in some areas of his life, God loved him and called him a man after His own heart because David desired the Lord. God was faithful to bring him into his inheritance, and even in David's struggles the Lord was faithful to keep him close to Himself.

Yes, David had some very big failures in his life. But when you and I think about King David, what do we think about? We think about the sweet psalmist of Israel. We think about the boy defeating the lion and the bear by the grace of God. We think about the faith of a young man who defeated the giant Goliath. We think about the one who could play his instrument and drive the devil away from King Saul. We think about the man who stayed faithful to the Lord even when he was pursued by his enemies day and night. We think about the man who danced before the ark of God as the presence of the Lord was being ushered once again into Israel. And we think about the one who at the end of his days was given the pattern of the temple that the glory of God was going to visit one day.

That's how we remember David because God put His honor upon him and covered him in His righteousness!

What the Lord requires of you and me is a heart that thirsts for the kingdom of God—a heart that recognizes that we are bankrupt and without strength to live the Christian life apart from God. The Lord has promised to be an everlasting source of supply so that when we are at the end of ourselves, it is the beginning of God doing the work in our lives. You see, that's what the apostle Paul discovered in life. When he is weak, then God is strong. When we come to the end of ourselves, then God begins the work in us that needs to be done. Our victory comes when we recognize that it's about God working in and through us and not about us "trying" to do what is right.

When self dies, Christ lives. That's why the Lord will allow things to come into our lives that exhaust our dependency on self. If you have come to the recognition that you are completely bankrupt and you can't be a Christian on your own, raise your hands in victory because that's when God's living water starts pouring through you! It will be something of joy that you've never experienced in your entire life. It will be something that makes you want to dance in the street. It will be something that will make you want to sing because suddenly it's all Jesus and none of you.

When I am weak, then I am strong!

That's the beauty of it all.

When Jesus was on earth preaching, most of those who were strong in themselves stood in the distance watching and analyzing Him from afar. Listen, it was the sinners, the weak, the lame, the blind, the poor, and the captives who pressed through to be near Jesus and to have Him touch them! And it was this same group of people who received God's touch and were set free!

All you need is a heart for God. The Lord wants to speak to your heart and be the power source for everything that you need to bring you into victory...to bring your family into victory...to bring your friends into victory...to bring your neighborhood into victory...to bring your community into victory...

The Lord says to you today, "I will be your God. I will be your power. I will be your authority. I will be your life."

<hr>

IMPORTANT TAKEAWAYS FROM THIS CHAPTER

KEY THOUGHT: The message of God to His people is there is a deliverer, and His name is Jesus.

KEY WORD: Freedom

KEY INSIGHT: People may marginalize you and even reject you, but God never does. His heart and passion in sending His Son into the world were for your deliverance and healing.

Chapter Ten

PRAYING FOR AWAKENING

DOES YOUR FAITH need awakening?

Instead of living the abundant, fruitful life that Jesus promised, are you living in a quagmire of slumber and defeat?

Never have believers had as many resources, tools, and places to fellowship as they do in today's society, yet in the abundance of these things we have never been more ineffective and lukewarm in our faith.

Why is that?

Revelation 3:14–19 says:

> And to the angel of the church of the Laodiceans write, "These things says the Amen, the Faithful and True Witness, the Beginning of the creation of God: 'I know your works, that you are neither cold nor hot. I could wish you were cold or hot. So then, because you are luke-warm, and neither cold nor hot, I will vomit you out of My mouth. Because you say, "I am rich, have become wealthy, and have need of nothing"—and do not know that you are wretched, miserable, poor, blind, and naked—I counsel you to buy from Me gold refined in the fire, that you may

be rich; and white garments, that you may be clothed, that the shame of your nakedness may not be revealed; and anoint your eyes with eye salve, that you may see. As many as I love, I rebuke and chasten. Therefore be zealous and repent.'"

We are rich and have need of nothing. In many ways this describes the church in America. It describes you and me. There is an abundance of Bibles to choose from—different translations, different study notes, and even designer covers. Some homes have multiple Bibles lying around—but how often are they opened? We can go online or to a bookstore and get all kinds of resources that help guide us in our daily walk. And yet we are largely still living with one foot in the Spirit and one foot in the flesh. There are megachurches on almost every corner in our communities, but we are more disconnected from one another than we have ever been.

Why is that?

Consider the following story that I read recently:

It is said that a certain guide lived in the deserts of Arabia who never lost his way. He carried with him a homing pigeon with a very fine cord attached to one of its legs. When in doubt as to which path to take, he threw the bird into the air. The pigeon quickly strained at the cord to fly in the direction of home, and thus led the guide accurately to his goal. Because of this unique practice he was known as "the dove man." So, too, the Holy Spirit, the heavenly Dove, is willing and able to direct us in the narrow way that leads to the more abundant life if in humble self-denial we submit to His unerring supervision.[1]

When African American and forward-thinking white pastors in Alabama streamed the services live from Times Square Church, they were astonished to see over one hundred ethnicities worshipping together in peace and Christian love. One glance at our choir loft confirms that. So the Alabama pastors contacted Times Square Church and asked me to come speak in Selma and bring our ethnic, multinational choir.

The evangelical rally in Selma was packed, the message God gave me to deliver was powerful, and there appeared to be genuine breakthrough. But afterward, when the mixed group of white and black pastors gathered together in the home of a prominent Selma socialite for a meal, the white pastors ate in the elegant dining parlor, and the black pastors ate on the screened porch.

It was as if no one heard the message—they simply left it behind when they left the auditorium. I was shocked at the seating arrangement and took my plate out to the porch and sat with the black pastors. This, I was told, offended our white, socialite hostess.

One lesson I learned from the evangelistic rally in Selma, Alabama, was that the need for spiritual awakening and unification exists in our own backyard in the United States. A pastor from Rwanda whom I know would have nodded his head and said, "You see? Preach and celebrate without carving the Word into people's hearts, and the old evil comes back."

⊷•⊷

What is spiritual awakening, and why do we need it so much? In simple terms, spiritual awakening is when a person's heart is open to the voice of God, is tuned in to hear Him speak, allows Him to rule over her life, and does not resist the words God speaks.

We live in an era when there is a lot of religion but very little relationship with God. There are a lot of Christian churches but not a lot of early church power and testimony. And there are a lot of "salvations" but not a lot of "lordship" and walking the walk.

Considering the fact that we live in a place with religious freedom, there are Bibles and books and resources everywhere to help us in our walk, and there are an immense number of Bible-believing churches and megachurches spread throughout the nation, we are profoundly weak in the faith and making little, if any, impact on our culture.

It's time to have a spiritual awakening...and it starts with you and me.

THE SIGNIFICANCE OF GOD'S VOICE

I want you to really think about the significance of God's voice in your life.

John 1:1–4 says, "In the beginning was the Word, and the Word was with God, and the Word was God. He was in the beginning with God. All things were made through Him, and without Him nothing was made that was made. In Him was life, and the life was the light of men."

Word in the Greek New Testament is *logos*, which means intelligent speech. I find this so refreshing. When we look around at our society today—especially the airways with all of its talk shows and the pundits sharing their opinions— we realize how much we could use intelligent speech in our culture. The Word of God is intelligent. When God speaks, it is filled with intelligence, truth, goodness, and knowledge.

In verse 3 of the previous scripture, it says, "All things were made through Him, and without Him nothing was made that was made." God's words were not only intelligent but also powerful. Think about the creation of the world. In the Book of Genesis we are told that the world was just an empty void until God spoke. The Spirit of God moved on the face of the waters, and God began to speak, and light was created, piercing the darkness. God spoke again, and dry land was divided from the waters. Then the Lord commanded living beings to come to life, and animals of all kinds, including birds and sea creatures, rose to life on the earth.

And then ultimately God spoke right into the dust of the earth and with His own breath created man in His own image. Nothing in creation resisted the voice of God. God spoke, and the elements obeyed. There was an awakening at the time of Creation. There was darkness on the face of everything until God began to speak, and out of nothing, the writer of Hebrews says, things began to be formed.

Would you be surprised to know that God still works that way today?

When God finds a heart that does not resist His spoken word, the miraculous begins to happen. Things begin to be created—life comes where there was only death. Spiritual awakening takes place when we choose to believe God rather than our circumstance, when we choose to believe what God's Word says rather than what we see in the mirror, and when we choose to hear and believe the voice of God rather than what people tell us.

In Mark chapter 4 we are once again given an example of the power of God's voice. Jesus and the disciples had a long day of ministry and were in a boat heading across the sea to the other side of the region. A terrible storm stirred up and started tossing the boat back and forth. The disciples were filled with fear. I imagine that it had to be quite a storm, considering that many of the disciples were burly fishermen. I wouldn't think they would scare easily. Interestingly enough, while the disciples were filled with panic, Jesus was peacefully sleeping through the storm!

The disciples cried out to Jesus and said, "Teacher, do You not care that we are perishing?" (Mark 4:38). Scripture tells us that He rose up, stood in the face of the storm, and said only three words: "Peace, be still!" (v. 39).

Instantly the wind stopped, the waves calmed, and the rain subsided. The disciples said among themselves, "What manner of man is this, that even the wind and the sea obey him?" (v. 41, kjv).

Remember, "in the beginning was the Word, and the Word was with God, and the Word was God"…and "the Word became flesh" (John 1:1, 14).

What kind of a man is this who has authority over the elements?

The Son of God, who by the power of His voice created the weather patterns when He created the world, has authority over the elements He created. You see, with the exception of mankind, all of creation can't resist the voice of God. When God speaks, He has both the power to stop certain action and the power to start other things in motion.

God's creation recognizes their Creator.

Out of all that God created, it is only human beings who can choose to resist God's voice. You and I are the only created beings who were made in the very image of God. The Lord has given us free will—we are not robots; we are able to choose how we respond to our Creator. But it is Jesus' desire that His people, who are called by His name, would recognize His voice and obey, believe, and trust His Word!

In the book of John, chapter eleven, we are given another account of the power and authority of God's voice. Jesus' friend Lazarus has died. When Jesus arrives at the tomb of Lazarus, He stands on the mountainside and looks at the scores of people who are grieving. The crowd is hopeless, thinking it was too late for anything to be done. Many of them feel remiss, thinking, "If only Jesus had gotten here sooner, He could have healed the illness that took Lazarus' life."

None of those grieving believed that Jesus could do anything to help Lazarus now—it was too late.

The Bible tells us that "Jesus wept" (John 11:35). It is the shortest verse in Scripture. Whether Jesus wept out of grief, or over the unbelief of the people, or at the human condition of sin, which causes death, we are not entirely sure, but we do know that He loved Lazarus and that His delay was on purpose so that they could witness the power of God even over death!

Jesus asks for the stone to be rolled away from the tomb. As the crowd, including the disciples, looks on, Jesus cries out in a loud voice, "Lazarus, come forth." Still wrapped in graveclothes, Lazarus comes walking out of the tomb. In spite of the unbelief that was all around Jesus before He called out to Lazarus, there was one person who could not resist the voice of God, and that was Lazarus. It was a dead man who heard the voice of God and obeyed!

When God brings awakening, we must stand in the gap and fill it. Years after the Burundi experience, I was sharing God's Word with some military and elected officials in Washington, DC. In our gathering there was a pastor from Rwanda. He told me, quite sternly, that we must never forget to teach God's Word, especially following a spiritual awakening.

There was a great awakening in Rwanda before the horrible genocide that took place there before our arrival in neighboring Burundi. In the Rwanda awakening the refugees from both sides of the Burundi genocide (who had fled to Rwanda) had the hatred and bitterness swept from their hearts. In what I am told was a marvelous spiritual revival, the refugees celebrated in the joy of the Lord. They danced. They sang. They celebrated God's victory with an outpouring of emotion.

But just as Jesus taught His disciples in Luke chapter 11, once a heart is swept clean, it must be immediately filled with the love, fear, and truth of the Lord, lest the demon returns with seven of his friends more evil than he. In Rwanda, according to the pastor who confronted me in Washington, DC, the refugees rejoiced in their initial awakening, but the pastors there had not taught the new believers the Word of God, and they were left without a foundation and without discipleship.

Soon demonic forces far stronger and more evil than before entered the clean hearts of the people there and aroused them to commit genocide on a scale three times larger than the mass killings in Burundi.

Unfortunately God's voice is not the only voice we hear. When God first created Adam and Eve, they enjoyed perfect communion with God—there was no sin and no resistance to the voice of God. That all changed when Satan entered the picture in the Garden of Eden. All of a sudden, there was another voice speaking to Adam and Eve, and his words, which were unintelligent, challenged the voice of God. How did Satan tempt Eve to resist God's voice? He twisted God's Word around and cast doubt on the Lord's goodness. He told Eve that the only reason God did not want her and Adam to eat the fruit of the tree of knowledge was because they would become just like God.

And it was the lies of Satan (remember, he also said, "Surely you will not die") that brought sin and death into the world. But it also brought other voices besides God's into the world and with that the ability to resist the true voice of God.

Just as Satan did in the Garden of Eden, the voices we hear today in our culture exalt themselves above the knowledge of God, resisting what God has spoken. We hear it all the time on our airwaves, in our schools, in our courts, in our communities, and sadly even in some of our churches. The voices say, "Has God said...?" "Does God really mean this?" "Is God really the last authority?" "Is there not another way to heaven?" "Can we not be as God?"

In the last days people will be captivated by voices other than God's—empty words of those who want their money and their admiration. The Bible clearly says that under their influence people will become servants of their own inner corruption (2 Pet. 2:19).

Second Timothy 3:2–5 says, "For men will be lovers of themselves, lovers of money, boasters, proud, blasphemers, disobedient to parents, unthankful, unholy, unloving, unforgiving, slanderers, without self-control, brutal, despisers of good, traitors, headstrong, haughty, lovers of pleasure rather than lovers of God, having a form of godliness but denying its power. And from such people turn away!"

A religion of *self* will be the religion of the last day. It will not be the voice of God. It will be unintelligent speech. The apostle Paul says that they will be turned from truth and instead turn to empty words—fables and stories—words that hold no truth or power.

Second Peter 2:1–3 says, "But there were also false prophets among the people, even as there will be false teachers among you, who will secretly bring in destructive heresies, even denying the Lord who bought them, and bring on themselves swift destruction. And many will follow their destructive ways, because of whom the way of truth will be blasphemed. By covetousness they will exploit you with deceptive words; for a long time their judgment has not been idle, and their destruction does not slumber."

GOD'S AUTHORITY OVER YOUR LIFE:
THE LORDSHIP OF JESUS CHRIST

Throughout history there have always been leaders and individuals in and out of the church who profess Christ's name but deny His lordship. They deny the fact that Jesus Christ has sole authority to speak into my life and into your life. They also deny that Christ has the right to govern us, guide us, and lead us in both a spiritual and practical sense.

If we are truly Christians, we have accepted Christ not only as Savior but as Lord as well. We don't resist what He speaks into our hearts, but we embrace it as the highest way of abundant life.

There are far too many believers who accept Christ as their Savior but deny His lordship over their lives. Instead of Jesus being on the throne of their lives, they still are in charge. And instead of solely listing to the voice of God, they are continuing to listen to the unintelligent voices of the culture, of the self-help gurus, of the prosperity teachers, and of their own fleshly voice.

Many in our culture emphasize "another way" above the ways of God!

The list is long, but these voices tell us that there is another way to achieve what only God can bring into a person's life. They tell us there is another way to find happiness, there is another way to be healthy, there is another way to be accepted into heaven, and there is another way to live out your values. In all these things the culture's voices tell us there is another way besides the way prescribed through the Word of God and by the mouth of Jesus Christ Himself.

Yet, as believers, we know that it is God's voice—His word—that is the truth and that we need to heed. When Jesus stood in the temple (as recorded in Luke chapter 4), He took the book of the prophet Isaiah, opened it to chapter 61, and read, "The Spirit of the Lord GOD is upon Me, because the LORD has anointed Me to preach good tidings to the poor; He has sent Me to heal the brokenhearted, to proclaim liberty to the captives, and the opening of the prison to those who are bound" (v. 1).

Jesus came to stop certain things that have been set into motion in your life. What things is the Lord talking about? First, of course, is your sin nature. He came to put your sinful nature to death and to give you a new nature—a godly nature that is born of the Spirit and not of the flesh. He has also come to stop the perpetual wrong conceptions, ideas, and thoughts that have imprisoned you in your life so that you can be set free through the truth of God's Word. Whatever condition you find yourself bound to, Jesus says, "I came to nullify these things in your life—to set you free!"

In other words, for those who are spiritually poor, Jesus has come to reconcile us back to God. He has come not only to give us eternal salvation but to give us abundant life in Him—no matter what our circumstances may be! The Lord has come to take away the poverty of your thinking. He has come to take you out of the place where you've come to believe that nothing will ever change, that nothing will ever be any different in your life. Jesus has come to open the treasure of God's light to sinful mankind. He's come to heal the brokenhearted—those who have had some kind of experience in their lives that damaged them and made them believe that they are always going to be under the influence of this horrible circumstance.

What is it in your life that needs the voice and touch of God?

Whatever it is, Jesus is saying to you today, "I've come to stop this in your life. I've come to stand up and speak to it and say, 'Peace, be still.' I can and will stop the roaring of this circumstance and experience in your life. I have come to stop the waves of sorrow that are rolling over and over in your mind. I've come to put an end to it—if you will just listen to My voice."

Jesus has come to preach deliverance to the captives; that includes every sexually addicted person, every drug addict, every alcoholic, every immoral person, and everyone captivated by something of the flesh and of the mind.

Are you struggling in life? I want you to know that the Lord has said, "I've come to put a stop to these things that have dominated your life. I've come to give sight to those who are spiritually blind—to open your eyes to the reality that God has come and that His mercy is now yours."

The Good News means that the freedom of Christ can be obtained by faith, that you can be saved from your sin and the curse of death. The chains of hell can be broken from your life, and you can be a new creation in Christ Jesus.

No matter what you face, the Lord has come to set you free from your bruised heart, from the darkness that surrounds you, and to get you out of the pit that you find yourself in right now.

Jesus has come to show you a way out and to stop the things that have governed your life so that He Himself reigns over every detail of your journey—both on earth and in heaven.

Now is your hour of freedom and deliverance.

Second Peter 1:2–4 says, "Grace and peace be multiplied to you in the knowledge of God and of Jesus our Lord, as His divine power has given to us all things that pertain to life and godliness, through the knowledge of Him who called us by glory and virtue, by which have been given to us exceedingly great and precious promises, that through these you may be partakers of the divine nature, having escaped the corruption that is in the world through lust."

God has not called you to just *survive* in this life—He has called you to be a wonder to your generation. Jesus has called you to live abundantly through Him—to enjoy His victory, no matter what your outward circumstances are, and to be a witness of His power to all whom you meet. He wants you so intertwined with Him that when people look at you, they acknowledge that God is alive in you!

———✦———

The Rwandan pastor who delivered the stern warning in Washington, DC, made it clear that we must teach the truth of God's Word to those who are recently spiritually awakened. To ensure a spiritual awakening is sustainable, it must be objective, not merely subjective. "My fear for you is that you will have a spiritual awakening in America like the one we had in Rwanda," he told me, "that you, like us, won't be ready for it."

It seemed odd at first that he approached me the way he did. But his words are like hot coals in my bloodstream to this day. If we pray for an awakening in the United States, as we have been praying for so earnestly, then we must be prepared to fill the hearts of the new and rekindled believers with the truth of God's Word. If God blesses our nation or any nation with a true spiritual awakening, it is our responsibility as keepers of the faith to teach the foundation of belief to every man, woman, and child.

Understanding the cross, redemption, regenerative life, and newness in Christ are basic to successful Christian living. If we don't prepare now to welcome the new and rekindled believers into our churches and immediately teach them the truth of God's Word, they will be awakened, excited, and revived—but the emptiness in their cleansed hearts will soon be filled with either God's truth or Satan's lies. As Bible-believing, Spirit-filled Christians, we may be all that stands in the gap and makes the difference in the lives of new believers. We must do everything God empowers us *to do to ensure that revival is objective and not merely subjective.*

━◦•◦━

The people who are going to stand in the gap and speak the truth in Christ while society tumbles down are not going to be superstars. They are not going to have entourages and trumpets announcing their arrival. Instead, they are going to be ordinary people who are walking in the power of God and serving those around them.

THE WILDERNESS—AN IMPORTANT PART OF SPIRITUAL AWAKENING

The truth is that ordinary Christians face extraordinary challenges. I don't write this to scare you but to encourage you in your walk with God. If, as believers, we have a concept in our minds that says we are not to have difficulties in our lives, then we are sadly mistaken. Throughout Scripture God's people faced incredible challenges, trials, and hardships. Our difficult circumstances in life are used by God to build our faith—to learn to trust in Him instead of ourselves and to let His strength carry us in our weakness. If every time a problem arises, we run around terrified, saying, "Oh, what will I do? Where is God in all of this? How will I get through tomorrow?" we will never truly comprehend who God is, understand how much He loves us, or enjoy His peace no matter what is going on around us. It's important that we learn, through our wilderness experience, to have that calm assurance that God is in control of absolutely everything, especially when things look hopeless.

The wilderness is a place where decisions are made. It's a place where character is formed and where God begins the initial work in our lives that will give us the courage to finish our journey on earth well.

Throughout scriptural history, people of faith, such as Moses, were made ready for God's true calling by having their own wilderness experience. In Moses' case, his lasted for forty years. And when God came to him and called him to set His people free, Moses was as far back in the wilderness as you can get. He was eighty years old, and in the natural you would figure his time to fulfill the call of God in his life was over. But because of his wilderness assignment Moses' call had only just begun.

The wilderness is a place that seems barren, a place that in our hearts we ask, "What possible good could come from me being here?" Have you ever said that? Have you ever gone into your prayer closet and asked, "God, what good could come from this? I'm in such a barren place. It's a place where there's nothing appealing to the natural eye. I don't like it here."

Have you ever prayed that?

In the wilderness there are no familiar landmarks. There's nothing to give you a sense of bearing. You can wander around and find nothing to tell you that you've been there before. The wilderness is completely unappealing to our senses. It doesn't smell good. It doesn't taste good. It doesn't look good. It doesn't sound good. There's only howling wind all the time. It's a place nobody is rushing to get into and everybody is rushing to get out of. Yet for some reason God takes us there.

Why would He do that?

I know about the wilderness, and I'm sure you are familiar with it too. I have been in the wilderness so many times I can conduct tours. Maybe you can too. The wilderness can be right in the middle of Times Square. It can be anywhere from a palace to a garbage dump. It begins when we are opposed. You see, we will be opposed whenever we begin to do what God has called us to do. Count on it. We'll be opposed by an enemy that is subtle. We'll be opposed by an enemy that is sometimes not so subtle. We'll be opposed with words, we'll be opposed with circumstances, and at times we'll be opposed by hell itself. And if we're not prepared for the opposition that's going to come our way, we will turn back in the day of battle.

The promises of God provide sufficient power in our hearts to keep us from turning back. The wilderness is a place where you and I begin to live by the promises of God and not by our own circumstances. We don't worship because we feel good. We worship because we've learned to trust in God and to praise Him no matter what life throws at us.

God promises that none of the plagues that touch the minds of the unsaved, who are driven by the wind and their sense of personal and social well-being—none of the plagues that are determined by the height of the stock market or the depth of their depravity—will affect us as children of God. We will be able to stand in the midst of the sea because we believe that God will make a path for us and that He will indeed work all things together for good.

Many people who have never been tested in the wilderness are going to crumble when the fiery trials hit. Churches are going to compromise and begin doing things explicitly against the Word of God because they have not been in the wilderness—they have shunned the classroom of Christ and have come up empty in their own strength.

In my youth I didn't understand why the wilderness experience was necessary in people's lives. I especially didn't understand why it was necessary in my life. If your journey is anything like mine, the wilderness will be a place where you will learn what it is like for old enemies to pursue and overtake you. You'll have nowhere to hide, nor enough natural strength to defend yourself. You will learn that you cannot fight the battle on your own. You will learn in the wilderness to stand still, be quiet, and let God fight for you.

The Old Testament documents time and again what happened to God's people when they tried to fight their battles in their own strength. They were defeated, and horribly so. Whenever the weakest and most unlikely warriors simply believed that God would fight for them—as He promised— the victory was won. Most importantly, when they didn't try to share in God's glory, He blessed them beyond measure.

The wilderness is a place where you and I will learn to trust in divine purpose. We will learn to trust in God. In fact, if we learn to trust God in the wilderness, He will provide to the point that even bitter things will become sweet. We must trust in God though the mountains shake and be cast into the sea. Though the seas roar and overflow their borders, we will not be moved because we have learned to trust in God. He is our strong tower. He is our shield. He is our hope.

You might be hungry and find the wilderness to be a very unpleasant place and moment in your life, but by trusting God in the midst of it, you will find that you will be sustained by His Word and you will be comforted by His Spirit. And though all of hell may seem to be unleashed on you, you will have that peace that passes all understanding because you have put your faith in the Lord.

Many believers pray, as Jesus Himself did, that this cup be taken away from them. But unlike Jesus, we pray that the wilderness experience would be passed on to the Christian sitting in the pew down from us! Some believers try to negotiate their way out of the wilderness with God. "O God," they pray, "get me out of here, and I'll serve You. Get me out of here, and I'll love You with all my might, heart, soul, and strength. Get me out of here, O God, and there will be no greater worshipper than me. Just get me out of this wilderness."

The Lord says to those of us who pray like that, "No, that's not My will for you." Of course Jesus knew that God's will and purpose for Him was to go to the cross, and He accepted God's will and lovingly carried it out. I'm afraid you and I, unlike Jesus, are more likely to keep arguing with God and saying, "How can it not be Your will to get me out of here, God?"

The reality is that God's will is for us to learn to give thanks *in* the wilderness—in the difficult circumstances of life where we find ourselves.

You don't have to go searching for God's will as if it were a needle in a haystack; it's clearly revealed in His Word. Many people I've known over the years have sat and waited for a unique calling of God that would set them apart from others— and a season in the wilderness is not what they had in mind.

They waited for a special anointing, all the while ignoring the will of God that was clearly revealed to them. Sadly they chose to resist God's voice and then wondered why their prayers went unanswered. Eventually these same people came to the conclusion that God doesn't speak to them, which caused great confusion and disappointment.

The bottom line is they didn't want to do what God wanted them to do. They didn't, in their natural flesh, want to go where God called them to go.

So don't despise where you are. Learn to thank God for the wilderness. Thank Him that He takes us to a place where His strength, healing, and power are manifested in our lives.

God Almighty is touched with the feelings of our weaknesses, and He calls us now to come boldly to His throne of grace to find help in our time of need. The Holy Spirit of Christ Jesus will provide us with courage so we can stand and not flee when it gets hard. We won't trust in our own strength but will instead stand still and see the salvation of our Lord. By His power, channeled through our simple belief, His victory will be won.

If You Can Do Anything?

In the Mark 9 story the father of the demon-possessed son asks Jesus if He can *do* anything for his son. Little did this dad know that he was asking the Creator of the universe and of mankind if He could do anything—if He had the power to help. Actually, as we have seen with the children of Israel in the wilderness who were guided by the word of God, this father simply needed Jesus to speak the word over his son, and the boy would be set free.

In Hebrews 4:12 the Bible says, "For the word of God is alive and active. Sharper than any double-edged sword, it penetrates even to dividing soul and spirit, joints and marrow; it judges the thoughts and attitudes of the heart" (NIV).

There are many voices in the world, and they are not without significance. But only the established Word of God is able to cut through all the voices in your head and give you the true voice of God. This father had heard the voices of the powerless disciples trying their best to cast out the evil spirit. Then there were the incessant voices of the scribes and Pharisees arguing with the disciples. I'm sure he had the voice of his own conscience speaking to him, not to mention the voice of the devil whispering lies.

Jesus, who is the Word of God, cut through all of the voices and commanded the evil spirit to come out and not enter the boy again.

THE NEED FOR SPIRITUAL AWAKENING

Jesus had called the multitude that had gathered around the father and his demon-possessed son a "faithless" generation (Mark 9:19). Jesus, in the same verse, immediately identified that their main problem was not only that they had a lack of faith in God and the One He had sent but that they refused to accept Him as their prime example of faith. Listen to what Jesus declared next in the same verse, "How long shall I suffer you?" (KJV). The term *to suffer* in the Greek literally means to lose patience. Jesus had continuously set Himself as the perfect example of faith, but that generation refused to accept His example. Jesus knew His physical presence was soon to end and they had but a short time to observe His life and accept Him as the One sent from God.

Jesus also knew that there would be subsequent generations after His resurrection that would believe the word concerning Him and experience a true spiritual awakening. This father of the possessed child had begun to believe the words of Christ and in a moment of an awakening cried out with tears, "Lord, I believe; help thou mine unbelief" (v. 24, KJV).

The work Jesus had come to do was manifest in his heart— precisely what the Lord wanted to happen, not only for this father, but for us as well. Jesus immediately commanded the spirit to leave the child, and the boy was forever set free. Oh, that this would be the testimony of all of us and that our generation would not be called "faithless" but "faithful."

Embracing God's Word and His Holy Spirit

Jesus tells us in John 16:13 that "when He, the Spirit of truth, has come, He will guide you into all truth; for He will not speak on His own authority, but whatever He hears He will speak; and He will tell you things to come."

The Bible is God's personal letter to you. It's your lifeline as a Christian. The words in that book are not just a historical account of God but the voice of God speaking personally to you. Every word in Scripture, by the power of the Holy Spirit, is yours. You have, with the power of Christ within you, the ability to receive these promises and to be changed more and more into the likeness of Christ!

The Scripture says to ask for the Holy Spirit, as He will teach you all things. You don't have to run to somebody for a word; God has given you all you need to know and hear in His Word. Dive into your Bible, and ask the Holy Spirit to make it real to you—to open your eyes and wake you up spiritually.

Don't live in darkness any longer, don't live in spiritual poverty, and don't live behind prison doors—God has set you free through the power of His Word and His Spirit, which resides in you. You're not called to lie in a corner and lick your wounds until Christ returns. You are called to be a victorious testimony of Calvary.

Pick up your Bible, and immerse yourself in God's powerful Word—I promise you, your life will change. Realize and grasp the incredible truth of God's voice speaking to you. This same voice that speaks to you is the voice that all of creation heeded. The same powerful voice of God who called the universe into existence is the same voice that speaks to you and creates a new life within—a life that is born of the Spirit. Don't resist of the voice of God in your life. Instead, believe and trust His

Word. If God says this is what I am, then this is what I am. If God says this is what I can do, then this is what I can do. If God says this is where I'm going, then this is where I'm going.

It was by the word of the Lord that Moses was sent on an impossible journey that was made possible by God Himself. In the same way, He calls you to an impossible journey. He's not looking to you for the resources to do what He has asked you to do. He's only looking to you for an obedient heart.

The Lord wants you to have an open heart and say, "God, I refuse to be bound by my image of myself. You've spoken words into my life—I'm getting back into the Bible. I'm blowing the dust off my Bible and immersing myself in Your Word so I can hear and follow Your voice."

Through the word of the Lord, King David was shown how to walk righteously in terribly adverse situations. The word of God is so powerful that only a whisper of God's word brought Elijah out of thoughts of self-destruction and into a place of continued abundant life. Josiah the king discovered the Word of the Lord as he set out to repair the house of God, and the Word of God brought blessing and righteousness for another season to the people of God. The apostle Peter found the direction he needed to guide him from impulsive spirituality to the rest that truth brings. And the apostle Paul was changed from being a murderer of Christians to a man who gladly accepted hardship in order to bring the truth of God's Word to the unsaved.

Christianity is not just a mental agreement with written concepts in a book; it's a supernatural life. God's Word is a living testament that when believed and heeded transforms our lives through Jesus Christ our Lord.

Will you listen to the voice of God, or will you resist Him? Jesus himself said, "My sheep hear My voice, and I know them, and they follow Me. And I give them eternal life, and they shall never perish; neither shall anyone snatch them out of My hand" (John 10:27–28).

⬦

If we truly heed His will for our lives and abide in Him, the church will explode into revival. I am convinced of it. There will be an awakening, perhaps beyond description. If serving in the cause of God's coming awakening, regardless of the cost to you, is truly the cry of your heart, Christ will reveal Himself to you as you've never known Him before. In this last hour in which we live—this last season of humanity as we've known it—we must pray for God to give all of us the desire to do His will.

Jesus asked His Father if it was possible to take the cup of the cross away, but He understood that it was the Father's will for Him to suffer the shame in order to save mankind. Jesus surrendered willingly and lovingly to the Father's will. We too must surrender to the trials and struggles God sets before us. In doing so, we must trust that His mercy and grace will be sufficient in the wilderness.

We must begin to boldly thank God for the awakening He will cause in our own hearts, in our cities, and in our nation. We must thank Him in advance for being merciful to this, of all, generations. Because of Him and Him alone, your life will be molded into His image and make a difference in your family, your neighborhood, your school, your business, and your community.

You will help fill hearts that have been swept clean of evil to be filled with God's love and everlasting truth. We're going into this storm whether we believe or not. But if we believe, we're going in with the power of God. We're going in together as the church of Jesus Christ. And after God has won His final victory, maybe I'll look across the lake from where I'm sitting and see that you have gone fishing too.

IMPORTANT TAKEAWAYS FROM THIS CHAPTER

KEY THOUGHT: When reading the Word of God, everyone would come to the revelation it is all about Jesus Christ.

KEY WORD: Awakening

KEY INSIGHT: A true spiritual awakening would first take place in your own heart and then in the church. The Holy Spirit has been given to us to lead us into truth, and truth to lead us into life.

EPILOGUE

I*T'S NOT ABOUT a book. It's about prayer.*
Throughout this book you have seen both the importance and power of prayer.

Prayer is the foundation of our relationship with the Lord—it is our communication line with the almighty Creator, the One who brought us into the world and who has a divine plan and purpose for us on this earth.

Prayer opens our hearts to the work of God in our lives. It becomes the air that we breathe—it sustains us, prepares us, and enlarges our understanding of who God is and who we are in Him.

When you "pray without ceasing" (1 Thess. 5:17), you are strengthened in the Spirit and realize that *nothing* is impossible with God.

———✦———

Driving down from Rochester, New York, one day in 2001, I was clearly told that our church needed to *pray*.

Shortly after, as our church prepared for a service, the

pastors fell silent, the people fell silent, and there was a stillness in the sanctuary that was indescribable. People didn't move, and they didn't speak—there was just an overwhelming presence of the Lord that kept everyone in silent prayer. It continued service after service and week after week.

We sensed the Lord was wanting to do something and that there was an urgency about it. Something was happening, but no one really knew yet what it was. The urgency was clear—we needed to turn to Him and focus on prayer rather than our usual outreach and programs. Though we still held our church services, we stopped all other programming, canceled all guests, put a hold on nonessential meetings and events, and focused entirely on prayer. And then the message came: pray for New York City!

We had no idea what was going to befall New York City, but we knew one thing: we needed to be ready for it. So in July of 2001 we began our intercessory prayer for New York City. God spoke to us about a season of hardship and that we needed to be prepared. So we prayed for strength and for the ability to serve God in the midst of whatever was going to come upon us.

We spent two months praying, interceding, and waiting on the Lord.

By God's grace, when the calamity of September 11, 2001, took place, our church was ready. I remember people coming into church ready to work—ready to serve. Our church body was calm and was able to help with the physical needs of those who were covered in ash, who were frightened, who were hungry, and who needed shelter.

Most importantly, our church body was prepared to give people hope. We were able to give people the spiritual comfort that so many in our city needed. The church was full on a regular basis, and we had a word for them from the Lord—one that drew people to Him in a time when fear and anxiety filled the city.

Not only was our church body able to help those who were flocking to the church for help, but we were able to help at ground zero as well. We had teams that stayed at ground zero night after night—feeding the firemen, police, and other authorities, and offering prayer and comfort to all who needed the hope of Christ in the midst of a national calamity.

God did a mighty work through His people during 9/11 because our ears were open to His voice. We prayed and sought the Lord for two months before the tragedy of September 11. And because of this we were prepared.

Let me ask you, Are you prepared for the difficult seasons of life? Are your ears open to the voice of God? Are you willing to heed His voice and commit to prayer?

One of the reasons I am encouraging you to pray is that I believe there is a hard time coming to this generation. We live in troubled and turbulent times, and we, as His people, need to be prepared not only to get through the dark days but to be the very ambassadors of Jesus Christ to all those around us who need the hope of the gospel. The Lord has His people—His church—here on earth for a reason: to be the feet of peace and the very heart of Christ.

It's time to pray.

NOTES

CHAPTER 1
PRAYING FOR SALVATION

1.   Mark Edward Moore and Jon Weece, *The Preaching of Jesus* (Joplin, MO: College Press, 2002), 57–58, accessed August 20, 2018, https://books.google.com/books?id=8pM7Rh6CuZgC&pg.

CHAPTER 3
PRAYING FOR STRENGTH

1.   James C. Howell, *Weak Enough to Lead: What the Bible Tells Us About Powerful Leadership* (Nashville, TN: Abingdon Press, 2017).

2.   Eric Fife, *Against the Clock* (Grand Rapids, MI: Zondervan, 1981).

CHAPTER 4
PRAYING FOR SERVING

1.   Viola Walden, compiler, *Sword Scrapbook II* (Murfreesboro, TN: Sword of the Lord Publishers, 1980), 100, https://books.google.com/books?id=teEv0GOxyRwC&pg.

CHAPTER 5
PRAYING FOR THE IMPOSSIBLE

1.   R. Kent Hughes, *Romans: Righteousness From Heaven* (Wheaton, IL: Crossway, 2013).

Chapter 6
Praying for Forgiveness

1. John M. Perkins, *Let Justice Roll Down* (Ventura, CA: Regal Books, 2006), https://books.google.com/books?id=cVslBQAAQBAJ&.

Chapter 8
Praying for Peace

1. "Peace Like a River," Grace & Peace, accessed July 12, 2018, http://gracepeace.net/gap/76.html?.

2. Caroline Davies, "Queen Sees the Happy Face of Trench Town," *The Telegraph*, February 20, 2002, https://www.telegraph.co.uk/news/worldnews/centralamericaandthecaribbean/jamaica/1385477/Queen-sees-the-happy-face-of-Trench-Town.html.

Chapter 10
Praying for Awakening

1. Tony Abram, "Manifestation of Children of God on Earth!," Sermon Central, October 30, 2008, https://www.sermoncentral.com/sermons/manifestation-of-children-of-god-on-earth-tony-abram-sermon-on-church-growth-128262?page=2.

A FREE GIFT TO YOU

What will change your life, your community, and the world? Prayer. I'm so grateful you read my book. My prayer is that you were blessed, and that you will share with others what I have imparted to you.

As my way of saying **THANK YOU** for reading my book, I'm offering you a couple of gifts:

* E-book download: *It's Time to Pray*
* Study guide: *It's Time to Pray*
* Video: *Five Powerful Sermons on Prayer*
* Video, audio, and PDF: *Thoughts on Faith and Prayer* from the Book of Esther

To claim these **FREE GIFTS**, please go to: ***itstimetopraybook.com/gift***

Thanks again, and God bless you,

Pastor Carter Conlon